# now *that's* funny!

## Jokes and Stories from the Man Who Keeps America Laughing

by Andy Simmons

Reader's
Digest

The Reader's Digest Association, Inc.
New York, NY / Montreal

**FOR READER'S DIGEST**
**U.S. Project Editor:** Katherine Furman
**Project Designer:** Jennifer Tokarski
**Managing Editor:** Lorraine Burton
**Senior Art Director and Cover Designer:** George McKeon
**Associate Publisher, Trade Publishing:** Rosanne McManus
**President and Publisher, Trade Publishing:** Harold Clarke
**Executive Editor, Reader's Digest North America:** Courtenay Smith
**Creative Director, Reader's Digest North America:** Robert Newman
**Editor-in-Chief and Chief Content Officer, Reader's Digest North America:** Liz Vaccariello
**President, Reader's Digest North America:** Dan Lagani
**President and Chief Executive Officer, Reader's Digest Association, Inc.:** Robert E. Guth

Library of Congress Cataloging-in-Publication Data

Simmons, Andy.
  Now that's funny : hilarious stories from the man in charge of making America laugh /
Andy Simmons.
    p. cm.
  ISBN 978-1-60652-500-5 (alk. paper)—ISBN 978-1-60652-504-3 (epub)—
ISBN 978-1-60652-505-0 (adobe)
  1.  American wit and humor.  I. Title.
  PN6165.S56 2012
  818'.602—dc23
                            2012008802

We are committed to both the quality of our products and the service we provide to our
customers. We value your comments, so please feel free to contact us.

     The Reader's Digest Association, Inc.
     Adult Trade Publishing
     44 South Broadway
     White Plains, NY 10601

For more Reader's Digest products and information, visit our website:
     www.rd.com (in the United States)
     www.readersdigest.ca (in Canada)

Printed in the United States of America

1  3  5  7  9  10  8  6  4  2

*This book is dedicated to my beautiful and devoted wife, Linda, who . . . wait, that's not her name. What's her name? I said it just this morning, "Hey, HER NAME, you ate the last Entenmann's crumb donut again!" It's a name with a "G" sound. Geronimo? No. Gulie? Wait, it's right here on page 59 . . . Salsa? No, that's not it. There's someone named Jennifer here . . . That's it! To my wife . . . wait, where's that page again . . . Jennifer! To my wife, Jennifer (JenniferJenniferJenniferJennifer, okay, got it). Who has good-naturedly allowed herself to be used as my unwitting dupe in so many articles over the years. That, or she never complains because she doesn't bother to read anything I write. In any case, she is beautiful and devoted and even laughs at most of my jokes. Okay, some. Okay, smiles appreciatively. All right, nods in recognition that my mouth is moving before she turns back to watch* Ghost Hunters. *Oh, what the hell, I love her. Now I'm blushing.*

# Contents

The Most Important Thing About This Book     8

**Part One: America the *Funny***     11

My Life as an Award-Winning Jokes Editor     13

America's Ten Funniest Jokes     20

Be the Funniest Person in the Room     27

America's Funniest Family Stories     31

Stand Up? Sit Down!     41

**Part Two: All in the *Family***     47

Welcome to My Life     49

Macho, Macho Man     52

The "F" Word     55

Ode to My Puppy #1     58

Lord of the Dance     59

Brush Up on Your Shakespeare     66

Yankee Doodle Andy     67

Ode to My Puppy #2     71

Making Up Is Hard to Do     72

"In Five Hundred Feet, You Will Be Lost"     74

"Plutonic" Friends     79

How to Ruin a Joke     82

Itching for a Fight     85

Buff Your Shoes with a Banana     88

How Sweet It Is     91

The Dow of Pooh     95

**Part Three: America the *Odd***     101

America, the Beautiful . . . and Odd . . . and
Hysterical . . . and . . .     103

My American Journey (Part 1)     105

Lessons I Learned from Dumb Criminals—
All Too True Edition     107

Liar, Liar     113

Calling Dr. Frankenstein!     118

Don't Call Us, We'll Call You     122

So Sue Me!     125

The Guide to the American Man-Hug     132

Lame Excuses     134

My American Journey (Part 2)     140

**Part Four: I Work with Other Funny People**     **143**

Let Me Get My Red Pencil     145

The Petrified Woman!     149

Humorist Jimmy Tingle Proposes an Alternative
to the Alternative to the Alternative Energy Plan     156

The Mad Men of Pranks Inc.!     160

What Does a Movie Producer Do?     168

Make It Stop!!     171

**Part Five: I Suck Up to Famous People**     **181**

A Q&A with the King of Ha-Has, Andy Simmons     183

Tragedy Tomorrow, Comedy Tonight:
A Chat with Woody Allen     189

The Funniest Person I Know: Carl Reiner
on Mel Brooks     194

Robin Williams Grows Up (Just a Little)     195

A Comic's World     203

The Funniest Person I Know: An Older Garry
Shandling on a Younger Garry Shandling     213

Stop Clowning Around: Alan Alda Says
the Joke's on You     214

Oy, It's the Holidays!     216

Mirth Mother: My Interview with Comedian
Anita Renfroe     217

The Funniest Person I Know: *The Office* Writer/
Actor B. J. Novak on Ricky Gervais, et al.     222

Acknowledgments     223

# The Most Important Thing About This Book

I wrote my first book when I was six years old. The title was *Me*, and it was a no-holds-barred look at its young subject (turns out he was a perfect angel!). It was one page, the perfect length—long enough for the reader to enjoy the then state-of-the-art crayon typeface, short enough for them not to get bored.

I mention this because when the book editors at *Reader's Digest* asked me to write a book covering my years as the magazine's humor editor here, I was already a seasoned author and confident that I could produce a quality one-page tome. After all, my first book sold out its entire print run of one copy, and I was more than confident that my father would once again rise to the occasion and buy another.

"This needs to be a little longer than one page," they said.

"Are you sure?" I asked. "One page is a perfect length— long enough for the reader to . . ."

"We'll need a few more pages because we want you to walk us through what it's like to be the humor editor of America's largest magazine. Tell the world how you choose the jokes and reader-submitted anecdotes that are among the most popular destinations in the magazine. Include essays you've written, as well as the interviews you've conducted with famous comedians. Who were the authors you most enjoyed working with? Who do . . . ?"

"Yeah, great. But let's first talk about my author photo?"

"Excuse me?"

"The photo on the book jacket. We are going to have one, aren't we?"

"We haven't really thought that far . . ."

"Well, I think we should discuss it."

"But we haven't even discussed what articles you might include in the book. Maybe . . ."

"I think if we have the author's photo the rest will fall into place. Now, what should I wear?"

"We see this as a multifaceted work, part memoir and part collection of articles you've written and edited . . ."

"Know what would be nice? A black and white photo. Very dramatic. Besides, I have a lot of black and white clothes. I don't look good in pastels."

"You've been here nine years, right? We want to hear all about your favorite jokes . . ."

"Although one year for Halloween I went dressed as an L.L. Bean catalog and won first prize."

"We also want you to discuss how the humor departments came to be, you know, 'Life in These United States,' 'All in a Day's Work,' 'Humor in Uniform,' and . . ."

"Should I wear a hat? Hats are in."

". . . what you look for when a reader contributes a gag about his or her life . . ."

"Would you be able to see my socks? I have a collection of very cool socks. They're hand-me-downs from my father. They all have holes in them, but don't worry, they're in the heels, so they'll be covered by the shoes."

"You wear hand-me-down socks?"

"My father has excellent taste in socks."

"We also want to hear about the many celebrities you edited or interviewed . . ."

"Where's the photo going to be? The back cover or inside the dust jacket? Will we have a dust jacket? Do books really get dusty? And if so, can't you just wipe the dust off on your pants?"

". . . like Woody Allen, Fran Lebowitz, Jerry Lewis . . ."

"How much are we going to charge for this book?"

"What does that have to . . ."

"If we charge a lot then we can afford a really good photographer. And makeup artist. Shouldn't I be over zits at my age?"

"   . . .   "

"Should I smile or should I be serious?"

"   . . .   "

"How about when I pose I set my chin on the backs of my hands, you know, pompous-ass style."

"   . . .   "

"   . . .   "

"   . . .   "

"Basically, I'm looking for a photo that will leave people thinking, Now that guy can write! Because, truth be told, I'm not sure the words in the book will do the trick."

"How about this, why don't you pull together your favorite humor articles from the past nine years, including interviews, essays you've written, and jokes you've run, as well as some explanation . . ."

"What about if I wore . . ."

"Let us finish! As well as some explanation about why you chose these pieces. And we'll handle the author photo."*

---

*See back cover.

# PART ONE

# America the *Funny*

# My Life as an Award-Winning Jokes Editor

In 2011, *Reader's Digest* humor editor Andy Simmons was honored with a Nobel Prize for his role in the advancement of the Jokes and Anecdotes Arts and Sciences. Here is the speech he delivered at the banquet.

I want to thank the Swedish Academy for finding my labor worthy of this highest honor. I feel that this award was not made to me as a man, but to my life's work of retelling old jokes and cribbing gags from the Internet. I am especially gratified to be here, as I love smorgasbords. Las Vegas has some nice buffets, but nothing like the spreads you have in your lovely dining establishments.

Although I am being honored for my labor, it is my forbearers who deserve the credit. The first humor pages appeared in *Reader's Digest* in 1943. Readers were sending in their amusing true stories in droves, and the editors here had a revelation: "Great! Cheap labor!" And thus was born "Life in These United States," the first of our humor departments, which was soon followed by "Laughter, the Best Medicine," "All in a Day's Work," "Humor in Uniform," "Graveyard Hoots," and "Salmonella Sillies." (Sadly, the latter two did not prove as popular as their sister departments and were discontinued after only seventeen and twenty-four years, respectively.)

One of the early stories: A wealthy New Yorker, dressed in the Abercrombie & Fitch version of What a Man Should Wear in the Wilderness, walks up to a laconic Maine lobsterman. "I see you are using fish bait for lobsters. You think it's good, do you?" he asks. The lobsterman shakes his head. "No, I don't. But the lobsters do."

Those who were able to recover from the hilarity responded, "Hey, I can do better than that!" Since then, we have been inundated. Twenty million true stories and jokes were sent to us over the years, one hundred thousand of which we've published.

When people find out that I am the king of ha-has, I always hear, "I don't care who you are, you can't park here." Which is then normally followed by, "How can I get published in the *Reader's Digest*?" Why, this very exchange occurred just the other day at my wrestling class. I had Maya Angelou in a stepover armlock camel clutch when she managed to grunt, "Mr. Simmons, I have a joke for your magazine, but I'm afraid you won't like it."

"Try me, Maya," I replied, loosening my grip just enough so that she could breathe. Here was her offering:

> Rabbi Goldman is preparing to address an academic group on the Talmud when there's a knock on the door. He opens it to find a gorgeous blonde in a flimsy dress.
>
> "Surprise!" she shouts. "The program head sent me here as a thank-you."
>
> "Rabbi Schultz did this?" he roars. "A man of God does this to a fellow rabbi?" He grabs the phone and calls Rabbi Schultz. "You sent me this woman?

Have you no respect for me, my family, for my reputation? I can not believe you would do such a monstrous thing!"

Just then, he notices the blonde leaving. "Where are you going?"

"I didn't think you wanted me here."

"Why? I'm mad at him, not you!"

Now we know why the caged bird sings—she can't tell jokes. The fact that Maya Angelou trades in bawdy jokes notwithstanding, some might detect a slightly—how should I put this—moldy scent. Our answer? Precisely! You see, like any Fortune 1,000,000 business, we at *Reader's Digest* rely heavily on product testing. Just as General Motors tests its cars for years prior to letting a customer get behind the wheel and crash it, we test our jokes before publishing them. But we have a far more rigorous screening process: Our tests last for eighty years, and they must survive joke books, Catskills comedians, and e-mails from your Aunt Birgitta who "just had to share it with you." Jon Stewart, Louis CK, Chelsea Handler—who knows how funny they really are, because their gags lack the test of time. Not ours!

> Just as General Motors tests its cars for years prior to letting a customer get behind the wheel and crash it, we test our jokes before publishing them.

Our anecdotes are a different beast. They are sent in by readers who are only too happy to share their most embarrassing moments with thirty million other readers. In fact, we demand that these anecdotes not only be funny but juicy, too. This is because we're gossips. That's right, we enjoy reading all about other people's oafish spouses, dim-witted kids, and lazy coworkers. We then run around the office saying, "You think *you're* nuts? Look at what this guy's crazy wife did!"

Before you start typing up stories about the time your husband tripped over the cat, know this: It's not easy to relate funny stories. Many fall under the you-had-to-be-there umbrella. That is, it's hysterical to everyone except those who have to read it. The anecdotes that do work, like these that I've run in the magazine, fall under three headings:

## Misunderstanding

Our first day at a resort, my wife and I decided to hit the beach. When I went back to our room to get something to drink, the hotel maid was making our bed. I grabbed my cooler and was on my way out when I paused and asked, "Can we drink beer on the beach?"

"Sure," she said, "but I have to finish the rest of the rooms first."

## Wit

"What is that sound?" asked a woman visiting our nature center.

"It's the frogs trilling for a mate," Patti, the naturalist, explained. "We have a pair in the science room. But they've been together for so long, they no longer sing to each other."

The woman nodded sympathetically. "The trill is gone."

## Relationship

For some reason, the bookstore clerk couldn't get the computer to recognize my preferred-customer card. Peering over her shoulder at the screen, I said, "There's part of the problem. It shows my birth date as 12/31/1899."

"That's right," my husband chimed in. "She was born in June, not December."

*   *   *

They're all short (so as not to bore anyone), they're relatable (I can see my husband doing something stupid like that), and they tend to end on a punch line (okay, time to move on).

But it's not enough to have a funny story; it must also be well told. Many people ask me how they can punch up their jokes or anecdotes. Why, this happened just the other day. I ran into the esteemed novelist John Irving. He was looking a little down so I shepherded him into a nearby bar and allowed him to buy me a drink—a Napoleon Brandy so top shelf the bartender required a small helicopter to reach it.

**First, I told him, read the best material out there—devour it, dissect, absorb it . . . then steal it.**

"Andy," he said.

"Mr. Simmons," I corrected him.

"Mr. Simmons . . . I've often heard you state that you're the greatest living humorist in the world."

"In the world? I believe I said 'ever.'"

"Ah, yes . . . ever. What tips can you share with me?"

So I shared with him my secrets—not all of them, but just enough to get another drink out of him.

First, I told him, read the best material out there—the funniest stuff ever written in the English language. Twain, Wodehouse, Mencken, Seinfeld, Cosby—devour it, dissect, absorb it . . . then steal it.

"Steal it?"

"That's right, why go to all the bother of making stuff up when others have already done the heavy lifting?"

"Second," I said, after ordering a second round, "when you write humor, make sure that the humor structure is sound. I suggest you begin with the punctuation. Before committing words to paper, figure out where the commas, colons, and periods go so that they look funny. Once you have funny punctuation, the rest falls into place. For example: "    ,    ?     ," — :  "    ;    !!!!!"

"Frankly, this is pretty good on its own. I wouldn't muck it up by adding words. Remember, at *Reader's Digest*, brevity is a hallmark."

I then stumbled out of the bar, into the street, and got hit by a car.

For all you potty-mouths out there, here's one more thing to keep in mind: Our jokes and stories have to be clean. You can't use words like $#&%$ or *&!%, and you definitely must never mention something like &#%$%&%.

Here's the sort of joke we like telling at *Reader's Digest*: "Why does the Easter Bunny hide all his eggs? Because he doesn't want anyone to know he's screwing a chicken."

Yes, that's the sort of joke we like telling in our offices but can't run in the magazine. If I did, I'd get a little note back from my editor in chief that says, "Oh, please!!!!!!!" The first time I saw that I took it to mean she wanted more. So I threw in jokes about the little old lady who lived in a stiletto heel and the one about the traveling salesman who was trying to make it with the farmer's cow. (When the farmer's daughter walked in and said, "I'll do anything for you," the salesman said, "Great! Hold the cow still.")

Turns out, I'd misunderstood what she meant. She didn't want those jokes. You see, we're a family-friendly magazine. And the family she had in mind was not the Mansons.

I said my five-year-old daughter told me all these jokes. My boss didn't care. She didn't want Simmons-family-friendly, either.

So part of our job in the humor department is to walk that fine line between what is funny and what we can print without overburdening our company servers with angry e-mails.

Now, it is time to put down our speeches, pick up our plates, and head over to the smorgasbord. Since learning of my prize, I have spent hours in my kitchen perfecting the art of pyramiding food atop a small plate, then balancing it until I reach my dining room table. The secret, I have discovered, lies in the placement of the Swedish meatballs. They must always top off the plate and should never be placed at the bottom beneath the *filmjölk*, *Varmrökt lax*, *filbunke*, or *jordgubbar*. My floor learned the hard way that once those meatballs start rolling, everything starts to teeter, and soon it's every *filmjölk* for itself.

# America's Ten Funniest Jokes

**It's mayhem. Amid the clamor of pickle trays and pastrami-bearing waiters, eight old friends have gathered for their biweekly lunch at Factor's Deli in Los Angeles. They're all talking over one another, and no one is listening.**

These eight comedy legends, ranging in age from their 60s to their 90s—and with about 522 years of comedy under their collective belt—meet every other week to kibitz, eat, and reminisce. But mostly they're there to exercise their comedy chops by cracking wise at every opportunity.

It's this group whom I've asked to choose America's all-time best jokes. I've winnowed down the thousands of submissions our readers sent in, and it's our judges' job to pick ten from that collection. Some of these comedy legends may or may not be household names, but they've either written, directed, or produced some of the biggest movies and TV shows ever. Here's my line-up of judges:

**Sid Caesar:** Introduced America to Mel Brooks, Carl Reiner, Neil Simon, and Woody Allen on his 1950s TV hit, *Your Show of Shows*
**Monty Hall:** Television producer and host of *Let's Make a Deal*
**Arthur Hiller:** Directed comedies like *The In-Laws* and *Silver Streak*
**Rocky Kalish:** Wrote for *All in the Family*, *Maude*, and *Good Times*

**Hal Kanter:** Bob Hope's chief gag writer, he wrote *Road to Bali* for Hope and Bing Crosby

**Gary Owens:** The voice of Rowan & Martin's *Laugh-In*

**John Rappaport:** Writer and producer for *M\*A\*S\*H*

**Matty Simmons:** Founder of *National Lampoon*; producer of *Animal House* and *Vacation*

It's a dream-come-true for a humor junkie like myself to be sharing the same jar of mustard as these guys. And as a humor editor, it's a career highlight. That is, if I can get them to read the jokes.

"Excuse me, excuse me!" I yell over the din. I begin handing out sheets of paper containing the gags. "Can we start with the jokes?"

Rappaport begins: "A guy goes to his doctor's office and says, 'Give it to me straight. I know I'm sick. How long do I have?' The doctor says, 'Ten . . .' 'Ten what?' asks the patient. 'Years? Months?' 'Nine . . . eight . . . '"

"That's a good joke. I vote for that one," says Hiller.

"It is a good joke, but it's not on our list," I say.

Rappaport peruses the list and offers to read the monk joke, which pits him against Hall, who also wants to read the monk joke. Instead of either reading the monk joke, they start telling their own monk jokes.

"Maybe we can read a joke from the list?" I suggest over the laughter.

Kalish taps a spoon against a glass of Dr. Brown's diet cream soda. "Point of order!" he shouts. That's what the guys yell when they want everyone's attention. It doesn't always work, but that's what they yell. "I'm going to read one," he says. "And remember, gentlemen, *Reader's Digest* is picking up the tab today, so you know what that means: Eat as much as you want."

## Joke #1

A man, shocked by how his buddy is dressed, asks him, "How long have you been wearing that bra?" The friend replies, "Ever since my wife found it in the glove compartment."

They all laugh, except Kanter, who sneers, "It's so old."

"It doesn't matter if it's old or not," I say. "The point is, is it funny?"

No one's listening, because the joke genie has been let out of the bottle, and the gags (none from our list) start flying. Simmons begins: "A grandmother is watching her grandchild playing on the beach when a huge wave comes and takes him out to sea." Caesar leans in to hear. He knows what's coming. They all do—it's their favorite joke from their stockpile of gags. "She pleads, 'Please, God, save my only grandson. I beg of you, bring him back.' With that, a big wave washes the boy back onto the beach, good as new. The grand-mother looks up to heaven and says . . . 'He had a hat!'"

> "It doesn't matter if it's old or not. The point is, is it funny?"

"Very funny, but I want to give you a line read," says Rappaport. "It should be 'He *had* a hat.'"

"No, no, no," says Kanter. "It's 'He had a *hat*.'"

"'He *had* a hat,'" insists Rappaport.

"Then she's too angry," Kanter counters. "She's not angry—she just wants the damn hat back."

"Who'd like to read the next joke?"

"'He *had* a hat?'" Simmons tries.

Owens finally launches into the next gag on the list, drawing it out for all its comic worth.

## Joke #2

A ventriloquist is performing with a dummy on his lap. He's telling a dumb-blonde joke when a young platinum-haired beauty jumps to her feet.

"What gives you the right to stereotype blondes that way?" she demands. "What does hair color have to do with my worth as a human being?"

Flustered, the ventriloquist begins to stammer out an apology.

"You keep out of this!" she yells. "I'm talking to that little jerk on your knee!"

"Great," I say. "Who'd like to tell—"

"You know, that reminds me of a true story," says Owens. "It was the '50s. The ventriloquist Rickie Layne and his dummy, Velvel, were onstage at the Copacabana. In the front row were some gangsters. Velvel starts insulting them. 'Hey, it looks like you slept in your clothes,' he says. 'Don't you make any money? Is that the best suit you can buy?' With each put-down, the mobsters are getting angrier and angrier. Suddenly, the owner of the nightclub, Jules Podell—a real tough guy—jumps onstage. He grabs the dummy and punches him so hard his head rolls off. Podell then points at Velvel's head lying on the stage and says, 'One more joke like that and I'll kill you!' "

"True story," says Kalish, corroborating it between guffaws.

"Can we read another joke?" I ask.

"Anybody hear of a guy named Evil Eye Finkel?" says Kalish. In the '30s, Evil Eye's job was to go to boxing matches and fix some boxer with the evil eye in hopes of jinxing him.

The contest has now been hijacked by tales of all the Evil Eyes the guys have known. That's when I remind everyone that *Reader's Digest* will pick up the lunch tab only if they actually judge the gags. The men swallow their pickles, pick up their pens, and begin bickering.

"You actually like that one?" Kanter asks Simmons after the latter voices approval of the bra joke. Simmons, in turn, points out that Kanter had little company when he voted for an ill-fated gassy-granny joke.

Here, now, the rest of the ten best jokes in America (in no particular order), as decided by our judges:

## Joke #3

In surgery for a heart attack, a middle-aged woman has a vision of God by her bedside. "Will I die?" she asks.

God says, "No. You have thirty more years to live."

With thirty years to look forward to, she decides to make the best of it. So since she's in the hospital, she gets breast implants, liposuction, a tummy tuck, hair transplants, and collagen injections in her lips. She looks great!

The day she's discharged, she exits the hospital with a swagger, crosses the street, and is immediately hit by an ambulance and killed.

Up in heaven, she sees God.

"You said I had thirty more years to live," she complains.

"That's true," says God.

"So what happened?"

God shrugs. "I didn't recognize you."

## Joke #4

Every ten years, the monks in the monastery are allowed to break their vow of silence to speak two words. Ten years go by and it's one monk's first chance. He thinks for a second before saying, "Food bad."

Ten years later, he says, "Bed hard."

It's the big day, a decade later. He gives the head monk a long stare and says, "I quit."

"I'm not surprised," the head monk says. "You've been complaining ever since you got here."

## Joke #5

A guy spots a sign outside a house that reads TALKING DOG FOR SALE. Intrigued, he walks in.

"So, what have you done with your life?" he asks the dog.

"I've led a very full life," says the dog. "I lived in the Alps rescuing avalanche victims. Then I served my country in Iraq. And now I spend my days reading to the residents of a retirement home."

The guy is flabbergasted. He asks the dog's owner, "Why on earth would you want to get rid of an incredible dog like that?"

The owner says, "Because he's a liar! He never did any of that!"

## Joke #6

Two men are hunting in the woods when one of them collapses. The guy who fell isn't breathing, and his eyes are glazed. The other guy whips out his cell phone and calls 911.

"I think my friend is dead!" he yells. "What can I do?"

The operator says, "Calm down. First, let's make sure he's dead."

There's a silence, then a shot. Back on the phone, the guy says, "Okay, now what?"

## Joke #7

A turtle is crossing the road when he's mugged by two snails. When the police show up, they ask him what happened. The shaken turtle replies, "I don't know. It all happened so fast."

## Joke #8

A man is walking in a graveyard when he hears the Third Symphony played backward. When it's over, the Second Symphony starts playing, also backward, and then the First. "What's going on?" he asks a cemetery worker.

"It's Beethoven," says the worker. "He's decomposing."

## Joke #9

A priest, a minister, and a rabbi want to see who's best at his job. So they each go into the woods, find a bear, and attempt to convert it. Later they get together. The priest begins: "When I found the bear, I read to him from the catechism and sprinkled him with holy water. Next week is his First Communion."

"I found a bear by the stream," says the minister, "and preached God's holy word. The bear was so mesmerized that he let me baptize him."

They both look down at the rabbi, who is lying on a gurney in a body cast. "Looking back," he says, "maybe I shouldn't have started with the circumcision."

## Joke #10

A poodle and a collie are walking together when the poodle suddenly unloads on his friend. "My life is a mess," he says. "My owner is mean, my girlfriend ran away with a schnauzer, and I'm as jittery as a cat."

"Why don't you go see a psychiatrist?" suggests the collie.

"I can't," says the poodle. "I'm not allowed on the couch."

# Be the Funniest Person in the Room

We at *Reader's Digest* like to offer a service angle whenever we can, the reason being that self-help books sell better than humor collections. Think of this particular chapter as Situational Humor for Dummies, except I would never call my readers dummies.

The first rule of writing is don't insult your readers. Actually, that's the second rule. The first rule is don't insult the payroll department. They'll sit on your check for months. "Oh, Mr. Simmons. I could have sworn we sent that check out eons ago. . . ."

The following are jokes you can use when you need to defuse certain awkward moments. It will guarantee that you will be perceived in a heroic light and deemed the funniest person in the room (to clarify—in a room with other people).

## Class Reunion

**Obstacle:** These people have seen you at your worst—braces, zits, and in gym class. You now have an opportunity to dispel old opinions.

**Goal:** Clever wordplay gags will mark you as an erudite person-of-the-world and not the dolt who thought the name of the great Greek philosopher was Play-Doh.

**Jokes:** What do you call it when two egotists butt heads? An I for an I.

What did the bartender ask Charles Dickens when he ordered a martini? Olive or Twist.

What's a shotgun wedding? A case of wife or death!
(Okay, that's enough.)

## Family Reunion

**Obstacle:** Good news—that Adonis-like cousin of yours who beat you in tennis, basketball, and swimming races? You just destroyed his high score in Tetris!

**Goal:** A self-deprecating joke will show everyone that success hasn't gone to your head, even though it has, and for good reason: You're the family Tetris king!!!!!!

**Joke:** The other day, I went to work with both ears bandaged. My boss asked what happened.

"I was ironing a shirt when the phone rang and I accidentally answered the iron instead of the phone!"

"That explains one ear," said my boss. "But what about the other?"

"The person called back!"

## Kid's Birthday Party

**Obstacle:** An audience of ladies, gentlemen, and children of all ages.

**Goal:** Telling a joke suitable for kids—and one that isn't so cute it makes adults ill.

**Joke:** What did 0 say to 8? Nice belt.

## Adult's Birthday Party

**Obstacle:** Someone you love is a year older and isn't happy about it.

**Goal:** Whether he or she is turning twenty or one hundred, celebrate the occasion with an insult. Deep down, while you never hear anybody admit it, we all love jokes about getting older. After all, getting older is the objective.

**Joke:** A man brags to a friend about his new hearing aid.

"It's the most expensive one I've ever had—it cost me $3,500!"

His friend asks, "What kind is it?"

The braggart says, "Half past four."

## Golf Outing

**Obstacle:** You've swung at the ball twelve times and all you've succeeded in doing is giving it windburn.

**Goal:** Time to step back and change the subject by telling a joke about a golfer with a greater handicap than yours.

**Joke:** Stevie Wonder meets Tiger Woods and mentions that he, too, is a golfer. "When I tee off," the blind musician explains, "I have a guy call to me from the green. My sharp sense of hearing lets me aim."

Tiger's skeptical, but when Stevie suggests that they play a round for $100,000 Tiger readily accepts, figuring it's the easiest hundred grand he'll ever make.

> Whether he or she is turning twenty or one hundred, celebrate the occasion with an insult.

"So when do you want to play?"

Stevie shrugs, "Pick any night."

## First Date

**Obstacle:** Do you have a sense of humor? If so, are you Seinfeld-funny or Vladimir Putin–funny?

**Goal:** You're doing two things with this joke: (a) trying to show your date that you're not a humorless dork, and (b) fishing around to see if he or she is a humorless dork. Since you have a lot to learn about your date in a brief period of time, stick with a one-liner. If you get a laugh, stay for dessert.

**Joke:** How many quarters does it take to play the new *Lord of the Rings* pinball game? None. It only takes Tolkiens.

## Thanksgiving Dinner

**Obstacle:** Your mother-in-law is doing it again: She won't stop talking about the time your spouse cried on Santa's lap at the age of sixteen.

**Goal:** Reduce your partner's anxiety with a joke that states the obvious: The woman may be pushy—but, hell, you're stuck with her.

**Joke:** A manager brings a dog into a nightclub to work. The dog is a brilliant piano player who knows all the standards. He's sitting there pounding out the notes when all of a sudden a big dog comes in and drags him off the stool and out the door.

The nightclub owner asks, "What happened?"

The manager says, "That's his mother. She wants him to be a doctor."

## Office Christmas Party

**Obstacle:** Nagging boss, crabby clients, looming deadlines ... If unemployment didn't pay so badly, you'd choose it as a career. You work so hard none of your coworkers have gotten a chance to know you. This is your one shot to shine.

**Goal:** Since office parties are all about booze, that means one thing: a bar joke.

**Joke:** How many drunks does it take to change a light bulb? Twenty-one. One to hold the light bulb and twenty to drink until the pub spins.

# America's Funniest Family Stories

**"I come from a stupid family. During the Civil War, my great uncle fought for the West."**

I can relate to that Rodney Dangerfield quote. While my family is my greatest source of pride (my grandfather stormed the Argonne Forest with only a slingshot and a nasty attitude!), they're also my greatest source of embarrassment (he did so wearing a pink tutu).

A few years ago, I dared our readers to share their funny tales about cranky kids, witty spouses, dim parents, and anyone else who made them fall out of the family tree laughing. Here are my favorite submissions. As you'll see, they broke down along subject lines that positioned them and their loved ones in a certain light.

## My Family Is Helpful

My thirteen-year-old nephew thought his gangsta outfit—low-riding pants and exposed boxers—made him look cool. That is, until his five-year-old cousin took notice.

"Nathaniel," she yelled out in front of everyone. "Your panties are showing." —LINDA McLEMORE

It rained in Phoenix for the first time in what seemed like eons. So when my wife and I took the car out, she was more nervous than normal.

"You are an excellent driver," she assured me. "Just beware of the *other* idiots out there." —STEVE JACOBS

When my father ran out of gas, he called my mother to pick him up in her car. They went to a gas station, filled a gas can, and returned to his car. After a few minutes, he got back into her car again. "We need to go back to the gas station," he said.

"One gallon wasn't enough?" she asked.

"It would have been if I'd put it in the right car."

—KENT T. CRITCHLOW

While doing a crossword puzzle, I asked for my husband's help.

"The word is eight letters long and starts with *m*, and the clue is 'tiresome sameness.'"

"Monogamy," he answered. —DONNA VAN NOTE

I knew that my husband's hearing had deteriorated after our friend—new to the city—asked where he could meet some singles.

"Well," said my husband, "I see them in the Kmart parking lot diving for fries."

"Dear," I intervened. "*Singles*, not seagulls." —REGEN ROSE

## My Family Is Philosophical

In fourth grade, my son had a huge crush on a classmate. So for Valentine's Day, he bought her a box of chocolates and took it into school. When I returned home from work, I found him on the couch eating the same box of candy.

"What happened?" I asked.

"Well, I thought about it for a long time," he said between chews. "And I decided that, for now, I still like candy more than girls." —KYM LOKKEN

My sister is a know-it-all who bristles at anyone's well-intentioned advice. But when our older sister gave her several clever tips, she was impressed.

"I have to hand it to Pat," she told me. "She really is smart. Not *Jeopardy!* smart; more *Wheel of Fortune* smart."

—TERESA BRUCE

After my daughter sat glued to the TV set for most of the day, I told her, "Do you know that the average American spends more hours per day watching TV than the average Olympic athlete spends training?"

She replied, "What's the point of all that training if no one's going to watch?" —DAVE KOLACZ

"When I married Donna, I could get both hands around her waist," said my husband's grandfather. Pointing at his full-figured wife, he boasted, "Now look how much I got. That's what I call an investment!" —KATHERINE EBY

En route to church to make his first confession, my nervous seven-year-old grandson asked me what he could expect.

"Confession is where you tell all the bad things you've done to the priest," I told him.

He looked relieved. "Good. I haven't done anything bad to the priest." —DOUGLAS MATOOK

## My Family Is Inquisitive

My three-year-old grandson was attending a birthday party for a friend when the friend's father sneaked off to take a shower before work. Halfway through, the father heard a tapping on the shower door, followed by the sight of my grandson peering in. Looking around the stall, he asked, "Is my mom in here?" —BILLIE CREEL

At the restaurant, a sign read Karaoke Tonight!

Grandma studied it before asking, "What kind of fish is that?" —GAIL COLLIER

The photo in the newspaper was of a squad car parked next to a small airplane that had made an emergency landing on a highway.

My fifteen-year-old daughter was impressed: "How did that cop get the plane to pull over?" —DONA PIERCE

As we drove, a road sign warned: Survey Crew Ahead.

"Great," my wife whined. "Now what are they going to ask us!" —DANIEL GIANGIULIO

Our friends Dave and Kristen have a precocious three-year-old. One day, Kristen chided Alayna for calling her by her first name.

"Stop calling me Kristen," she said. "I want you to call me Mommy, not Kristen."

Alayna looked confused. "But Dave calls you Kristen."

—BELVA HUMBLE

## My Family Is Insightful

After she tripped and hurt herself, my sister filed a lawsuit. While she was being deposed, the opposing attorney asked, "Since your injury, is there anything you cannot do now that you did before the injury?"

"Yes, I can't ride my bicycle anymore," she said.

"And why is that?"

"Because it has a flat tire." —BRYAN HUGHES

I found my young son sobbing into his pillow after his pet toad died, so I reminded him, "It's not the end of the world." Through his tears he blubbered, "It is for my toad."

—MICHAEL GESSEL

My wife's family was cooing over our newborn when someone mentioned that the baby looked like me.

"Don't worry," said my mother-in-law. "She'll change."

—RAY OST

The morning he began kindergarten, I told my son about the great adventure that awaited him. "You're going to learn so many things," I said, "like how to read and write!"

When I picked him up from school later, I asked how it went.

"Well," he said, "I still can't read or write." —DEBBIE CRISS

## My Family Holds Grudges

After learning that her parents were in a minor car accident, my wife called her mother. "What happened?" she asked.

"I was driving and fell asleep," said her mother, irritated. "And of course, your father wasn't paying attention!"

—GUY LAMBERT

My husband used to work the night shift, so in the evening my five-year-old would climb into bed with me. One night, my husband came home early. "That's *my* wife," he joked. "Get in your own bed."

"Fine," grumbled our son, as he stormed off. "When I have a wife you can't sleep with her, either."

—KATHRYN BUCHERT

While playing Scrabble at my future in-laws' house, I asked my soon-to-be wife, "Is 'nag' a word?"

As my father-in-law walked by, he answered, "In about six months it will be." —MATT HILBURN

"He's going to beat me up!" yelled my four-year-old.

"Why would your brother do that?" I asked him.

"Because I accidentally dropped his toothbrush in the toilet."

"Just tell him and give him a new one."

"I can't."

"Why?"

"He's in the bathroom brushing his teeth."

—KATRINA STANFORD

## My Family Is Practical

At day care, my four-year-old watched as a teacher pulled something hot from the oven.

"What's that on your hand?" he asked.

"An oven mitt," she said. "It keeps me from getting burned. Doesn't your mother use them?"

"No, my mom's just really careful when she opens the pizza box." —JESSICA DODGE

"Sorry your card won't arrive in time for your birthday," my sister said to me. "I bought a belated birthday card, so I had to wait a few days before mailing it." —LINDA LEE

A gorgeous white convertible pulled up next to our parked car. "How did that woman get such a pretty car?" my daughter asked.

I recognized the driver and said, "Her husband's a pilot. He must make a good salary."

"That's what I want to be," she said.

"Really? A pilot?"

"No, I want to be married to one." —JEREMY JAMES

Shortly after Dad retired, my mother asked him, "What are you going to do today?"

"Nothing," he said.

"That's what you did yesterday."

"Yeah, but I wasn't finished." —BEVERLY SHERMAN

I was on the couch nursing my newborn when my three-year-old plopped down to watch. Seeing this as a good teaching moment, I explained how mothers feed their babies. My daughter's eyes grew wider with each detail.

"She's drinking milk?" she asked. "In the living room?!"

—BEVERLY FRIEND

## My Family Is Clever

I was not thrilled with the idea of letting my clueless thirteen-year-old son babysit his younger sisters, even though he begged me to.

"What about a fire?" I asked, referring to my number one concern.

"Mom," he said, rolling his eyes, "I'm a Boy Scout. I know how to start a fire." —JO WALKER

After she fainted, my mother was raced to the hospital. Her doctor asked, "Why do you think you passed out?"

Looking at him oddly, Mom replied, "Because I woke up on the floor." —JEFFREY WARD

Over dinner, I explained the health benefits of a colorful meal to my family.

"The more colors, the more variety of nutrients," I told them. Pointing to our food, I asked, "How many different colors do you see?"

"Six," volunteered my daughter. "Seven if you count the burned parts." —ALLISON BEVANS

Our three-year-old daughter was making up a poem when she asked us what rhymed with stop.

My husband said, "Think of something that's cool and refreshing, but that Mom and I don't let you drink."

Our daughter knew the answer: "Alcohol!" —JUDY BERKSETH

## My Family Is Upbeat

My two sons, Jake and Austin, are a handful. So I wasn't surprised that Dad looked frazzled after we took them to a football game. "It will be a cold day in Hell before we come to another game," he muttered.

"Did you hear that?" Jake shouted to Austin. "Grandpa's going to take us to a game in December!" —DREW SPECHT

At age seventy, my grandfather bought his first riding lawnmower.

"This thing is great," he bragged to my brother. "It took me only an hour and a half to mow the lawn. It used to take your grandmother two days to do it all." —DIANE HARDY

"Everything's starting to click for me!" said my father-in-law at dinner. "My knees, my elbows, my neck . . ."

—KATHRYN SEIFERT

The sight of my mother cleaning her dentures fascinated my young son. He sat riveted as she carefully took them out, brushed and rinsed them, then popped them back in.

"Cool, Grandma!" he said. "Now take off your arm."

—BARB SIPE

## My Family Is Tactful

A customer at a coffee shop was clearly peeved by the text message he'd just received. "You ever have that ex-girlfriend who just won't go away?" he asked his friend.

"Yeah," came the reply. "My wife." —JAMES BAVA

When my wife was a teenager, she desperately wanted to wear makeup. Her mother said no, so she appealed to her father.

Ever the diplomat, he reasoned, "Well, if the barn needs paintin'..." —LONNIE BURGER

A fourth marriage meant yet another name change for me. I didn't realize the upheaval it had caused until I asked my father why I hadn't heard from him in awhile.

"I forgot your phone number," he said.

"You could've looked it up in the phone book."

"I didn't know what name to look under." —CAROL MARSH

## My Family Is Loving

My sister, a religious woman, lives in a small, conservative community with her husband and basset hounds. Knowing how much she adores those dogs, her husband bought her vanity license plates.

My sister's pleasant surprise turned to horror when she took the plates out of the box and read BSSTLVR.

—CATHY HEIZELMAN

My daughter loved the picture frame her five-year-old son bought her for Mother's Day. She found a photograph of him and replaced the cat photo that came with it.

Landon became upset: "Why are you putting a picture of me in there when I bought you a picture of a cat?"

—LORI FEENEY

The day I knew my in-laws had finally accepted me:

As we pulled into their driveway, my father-in-law was on the phone. "Oh, I have to run," he told the person on the other end. "My daughter-in-law and her husband just arrived." —KATHY DIERKER

# Stand Up? Sit Down!

It's not too intimidating for an aspiring performer to wait his turn for the stage at the Comic Strip Live, the renowned comedy club in New York City.

The walls are plastered with photos of previous acts—guys named Carlin, Rock, Sandler, Chappelle. Jerry Seinfeld's scorecard when he auditioned for a spot is up there, too. He passed.

As I imagined my picture up on the wall, a thought crossed my mind: *Am I nuts!?! What am I doing trying to follow these guys?* My eyes darted toward the front door. There was still time for me to run screaming from the club. Then I heard it—my intro from the emcee, a stranger to my act: "Ladies and gentlemen, put your hands together and welcome a very funny man, Andy Simmons!"

I gulped for air like a largemouth bass on a hook. Then I headed toward the stage. It was showtime!

When I first walked into the Comic Strip eight weeks earlier, I was a carefree man there to take a few comedy classes. My classmates were an eclectic group. There was Glen, a social worker and Orthodox Jew; Andrew, a former Marine who saw action in Somalia during the Black Hawk Down days; Christopher, a gay Mormon who honed his comedy playing the role of peacemaker in his family; and Mike, who is deaf and has cerebral palsy and a speech impediment.

Our teacher was D. F. Sweedler, a veteran comic who has appeared on *Letterman*. He told us that over the next two months we would create a five-minute act, which would culminate in a performance onstage before an audience.

"Where do we find our ideas?" someone asked.

Everyday life is fodder, he told us. Family, relationships, fears. "Anything you would tell a psychiatrist. Anger is always a good source. Even if it's petty, make mountains out of molehills."

This worked for me. What I lacked in talent, I more than made up for in anger. My problem might be quantity over quality.

Working with my anger, I wrote a rebuke of an outrageously expensive restaurant I'd just gone to. Here's a choice snippet: "Rule number one: If a restaurant has a sommelier, you can't afford it. After my meal I realized that if a restaurant serves food on a plate rather than in Styrofoam, I can't afford that either. The restaurant is a converted barn. So when our stable boy hitched us up to our trough . . ."

"What are you talking about?" D. interrupted during the second class. "No one knows what a sommelier is."

"A sommelier is . . ."

"Yeah, I know what a sommelier is. But no one else does. And if this is a nice restaurant, why are you hitched to a trough?"

"Because it's funny?"

The following came at me as if shot from a Gatling gun: "Too detailed . . . overwritten . . . not clear what's going on . . . too fast . . . not funny . . . no . . . throw it out . . . someone else get up there . . ."

"It's all about the joke," D. implored. "Get in and get out. Whatever you don't need, cut. Rework this bit. Try making it more relatable."

\* \* \*

"We're not still at the restaurant, are we?" D. asked when I took the stage the next class.

"I'm afraid so," I said.

Poor D. I could see his spirit leave the room.

During the previous week I'd gotten rid of any mention of sommeliers and feeding troughs. Instead, I worked on making the skit relatable. So I opened with "Who here eats food?" Silence.

I soldiered on. I'd given my expensive restaurant a name: Le Second Mortgage. I then went on to say, "I ordered the octopus. Or to quote the menu, 'An inkling of octopus served with a rumor of shiitake mushroom, bathed in a notion of seaweed and a suspicion of asparagus.' In other words, I ordered an empty plate.'"

This class went better than the first. "Le Second Mortgage" was a keeper, the octopus gag was chum.

D. found another problem. "What's with your delivery?" he asked. "You sound like Alan King."

He was right! I had an old-timey way of telling jokes, like some vaudevillian opening for a trained seal act. Up-and-coming comics fall back on the shtick they were reared on. Growing up in the '60s and '70s, I guess I saw myself on stage in Vegas, wearing a tux and pinky rings, holding a scotch, and opening for Vic Damone. D. wanted me to be myself. One problem—I didn't know what that was.

So I went home to practice my material in front of a mirror. Maybe I'd find myself there.

"A pal of mine got pulled over for DUI," I said to my

appreciative audience. "Yeah, he's a multitasker. He can drink, drive, and crash all at the same time."

Working in front of a mirror didn't help. All I could think was, *I have Grandpa's nose hairs!* I spent the next fifteen minutes trimming nose hairs before phoning Eddie Brill. If I wanted to be a comic, I needed to know what all the great ones had in common. Eddie—the guy who warms up Letterman's audience—was the man to tell me.

"There are three things great comics share," he said. "They're honest, vulnerable, and they're not looking for approval."

I had the vulnerability part down in spades. As for honesty, to paraphrase George Burns, I can fake that.

"But what about the audience?" I whined. "I crave their approval."

"If you have fun, they'll have fun," Eddie said. "And if they talk during your set, do what I do. Lean over and say, 'Don't you hate it when you come here for a chat and they build a comedy club around you?'"

My classmates and I watched anxiously as the club filled up. Earlier, D. had warned me against overly high expectations. "Don't expect to kill," he said, using comedyspeak for doing boffo. "I'll be happy if you go up there, don't trip, don't forget the material, and get even one laugh." Frankly, I'd set loftier goals for myself than not tripping.

Andrew was up first and immediately forgot half his act. But he turned that into his act and the audience ate it up. Mike followed, and the audience reacted warmly. Then it was my turn.

Hearing my name, I waded through the room, where I passed an old friend. He smiled and gave me a thumbs-up. I climbed onto the stage. The crowd seemed friendly enough, at least those who were paying attention. (What was it Eddie told me to say?) "You know," I sputtered, "you really have to be a people person to be a bathroom attendant." For some reason they found that funny.

What they didn't find funny was the riff about drinking wine at my expensive restaurant: "The wine was just pressed. It was so fresh you could still taste the feet." And by the time I'd tossed in a line about illegal aliens, the audience had transformed into a roomful of Edvard Munch models, their silent screams begging for someone to give me the hook and then bash me over the head with it.

As I left the stage to polite applause, my friend handed me a drink. "Drown your sorrows," he said.

Here's the checklist: I didn't blow my lines, not most of them, anyway. I didn't sound like Alan King. I didn't fidget, flop sweat, or sob for my mother. I got through it. But I didn't kill. I know D. said not to worry about it, but let's face it, "killing" is why we took this class.

The fact is I don't belong on stage. I prefer telling jokes from the safety of my computer keyboard. This way, if I bomb, I won't have to hear about it until I get fired. It's better to get fired once than a thousand times on stage.

PART TWO

# All in the *Family*

# ! Welcome to My Life

**"Why would anyone possibly want to read about me?" I asked my boss.**

She had just asked me to fill in as a guest writer for Mary Roach who, needing to take a break from ragging on her home life, was on hiatus from her humor column, "My Planet."

"I doubt they would be, but we can't publish a magazine with blank pages," she said. And thus began my writing career at *Reader's Digest*.

Okay, she didn't really put it that way, but that was the impression I got. Fine by me, I thought. Everyone's convinced that their family is crazier than everyone else's, and I'm no different. Time to settle some scores! But where to begin? The fact that my wife and I choose foods based on their vitamin content? (She's a folate fan while I lean toward riboflavin because it sounds like it should taste better.) Or maybe it's the fact that my nine-year-old daughter, Quinn, still doesn't know how to close the Chinese takeout containers so that my Singapore mai fun doesn't end up cold. Or my father's insistence on sending unsolicited advice to the New York Mets front office. Or my biggest bugaboo: presents.

Ahh!

An eBay survey states that sixty percent of Americans receive unwanted or unneeded gifts during the holidays. Personal experience tells me that figure is low. My family loves to give presents; we just don't know how.

For example, my sister is the queen of what we've termed *inconsequentia*—gifts you never knew existed, needed, wanted, or knew what to do with. We have her to thank for our olive de-pimento-izer.

"A what?" I asked, turning it this way and that, and back to this again.

"An olive de-pimento-izer. Some people don't like pimentos in their olives. This tool will remove the pimento.

"Why not just buy olives without pimentos?"

"That's a lot of bother when this will do it for you. Don't get it too close to your face, it may also remove eyes."

It's not so much that she's giving *us* gifts; it's as if she's giving gifts to our attic.

At least my sister spends time searching for a gift for us to forget about. Not so with my brother, who annually takes home the trophy for Laziest Gift Giver. He never knows what to get anyone, so he pokes around your home and buys you something you already have—this way he knows you'll like it. Last year he bought me the book *Freakonomics*. "I know you liked it when you read it before," he told me. "So I got you another copy."

My attic is now reading it.

When it comes to our daughter, I like to get her educational gifts, or at the very least something that points her in the right direction in life—like a doctor's kit or a My First Goldman Sachs CEO Corner-Office Play Set. Not so my wife. She's of the opinion that our daughter ought to enjoy the present she gets, which is why this year she let Quinn pick one out herself—a pint-sized cleaning cart. It came complete with mop, bucket, feather duster, broom, and rags, fulfilling every father's dream that their daughter wants to grow up to become a hotel maid.

Of course, no one is harder to buy a gift for than my wife—the experience is fraught with traps. For example, Jennifer looks cute in hats. But if I were to buy her one, there's a good chance she will mistake my intention and assume

**I like to get her educational gifts . . . like a doctor's kit or a My First Goldman Sachs CEO Corner-Office Play Set.**

there is something wrong with her hair that requires it to be hidden. If I buy her a gift certificate for a massage, she might interpret that to mean I think she's so fat that I don't want to put my hands on her. In the end, I get so flustered I get her an olive de-pimento-izer and am done with my shopping.

In fact, the only person in my entire family who gives a gift of any real worth is my grandmother, who still cuts me a $10 check every birthday.

Most of the following pieces in this chapter have appeared in the magazine, while some have never seen the light of day. But they each have something in common: my family. After all, as I've said previously, they're my greatest source of amusement.

# Macho, Macho Man

What timing! I'd just worn a hole through my silk shirt and used up the last of my lavender-infused shaving gel when I got the memo that "metrosexual" was out and "machosexual" was in.

Women, it seems, have tired of men with hairless chests, so they've changed the rules: The old macho is back in vogue. From now on, guys need to look and act tough—at a minimum, tough enough to open jelly jars without having to run them under hot water.

Taking my marching orders, the first thing I did was exhale for the first time in three years—letting my belly settle back into its natural position draped over my belt. I then canceled my membership in the Tiramisu-of-the-Month club.

Gone, too, was the easy sympathy I doled out to my three-year-old daughter after she pulled the head off her Polly Pocket doll for the twelfth time. "Now it's a Marie Antoinette doll," I told Quinn, knowing that tough love was the best love.

Gone was my simple acquiescence when my wife, Jennifer, informed me we'd be watching the Melissa Gilbert retrospective on Lifetime Television.

"Sorry," I told her, "this TV has been reserved for a special edition of *Killing Cattle with Mike Ditka*."

Part of the machosexual compact is to fulfill traditional male roles—to be the rock, the decision-maker. So as commander in chief of our little tribe, I canceled our family trip to Hersheypark. "Machosexuals," I explained, "don't have chocolaty good times. We have adventures." But being a benevolent dictator, I presented an alternative.

"Who wants to go bareback rhino racing in Zimbabwe?" I asked.

Machosexuals are a patient lot, so when Jennifer said, "No, we're going to Hersheypark," I knew that perseverance was in order.

"Wanna take a steam bath in an active volcano in Indonesia?"

"No."

"Fly a MiG-29 at Mach 3 over Moscow, going sixty-thousand feet straight up in the air at a ninety-degree angle until the engine stalls and we tumble back to earth in a free fall, coming just ten feet off the ground before pulling up?"

"No."

"Kayak down Victoria Falls? Go skinny-dipping in the Arctic? Walk over to the mini-mart and eat five-day-old sushi?"

No, no, and no.

"You don't like to have fun, do you?"

Click! Jennifer turned on the TV and raised the volume until Melissa Gilbert's voice drowned mine out.

**Then, after much wrestling over the remote, we agreed that I should be kicked out of the house.**

Then, after much wrestling over the remote, we agreed that I should be kicked out of the house.

So off I stomped to the nearest watering hole to be with my fellow bulls. I was glad to see everyone had read the same memo as me. Gone were the cosmopolitans and chocolate martinis. In their place was only one choice: "Barkeep," I said, "gimme a Milwaukee's Best!" A cold, frothy one appeared before me.

There was backslapping, swearing, and a quick debate on wearing helmets while motorcycling. (Everyone was against it.) And we used the old bar-food favorite, edamame beans, to throw at a poster of Brad Pitt.

After raising a glass to the machosexuals of yore— Bogie, Duke Wayne, Attila the Hun—we took out our knives and whittled some sticks before calling it a night.

Back home, I snuck into the house to avoid Jennifer. We machosexuals pick our battles and in so doing know that tiptoeing is not the same as retreating.

In the living room, I found Quinn crying over her headless doll as Jennifer struggled with duct tape.

I grabbed some glue, and Jennifer handed me the doll. I reattached the head as best I could. It slipped a bit before drying, giving it that cock-eyed, self-assured look that's so attractive in a plastic doll. Quinn climbed into my lap, and the three of us played with her Polly Pockets.

Who knew playing with dolls could be so much fun?

# The "F" Word

## Honesty is overrated.

A few years back, I came home to find my wife, Jennifer, in tears.

"What's wrong?" I asked.

"Quinn used the 'F' word." She was referring to our foul-mouthed three-year-old.

"You mean—"

"Yes. She called me fat!" Jennifer is not overweight, but like most women I know, she has an inflated view of her body. She cautiously walked over to a full-length mirror and sighed. "Great, the only part of me that's trim is my breasts. Be honest . . ." Uh-oh. "Am I fat?"

"Not particularly." I tried to catch the words and stuff them back into my mouth, but they were quick, juking and jiving from my grasp until they landed with a thud inside her ears.

"Listen, Slim, you could stand to lose a few tons yourself!" she said as she stomped off toward the kitchen.

"I like my fat!" I said. "And remember, I've known it longer than I've known you. What are you doing?" The refrigerator door was open, and she was flinging pizzas, Hot Pockets, frozen waffles, and ice cream out the window.

"I'm going on a diet, and I'm dragging this family with me!"

"No, not the Chun King!" Too late.

The next morning, we waddled off to the bookstore, where the sheer volume of diet books demanded that we split up. I took the books between forty-one degrees longitude, fifty-five degrees latitude and forty-three degrees longitude, fifty-seven degrees latitude. Jennifer covered the rest.

There were low-fat diets, high-protein diets, low-calorie diets, high-fiber diets, water diets, vegan diets, fish diets, fruit-juice diets. There were books on portion control and books that screamed, "EAT LIKE A PIG!" on the cover. Overwhelmed, we settled for just one shelf's worth. We'd try a different diet every day for a month until one worked. We dubbed it the Diet-a-Day Diet.

First up was the color diet. You can eat all the food you want, as long as it's one hue.

"Let's try brown," I said. "We can have steak, fried mozzarella sticks, stout ale, hash browns, and chocolate cake. As long as we don't eat a salad, we're fine."

Jennifer thought choosing brown smacked of cheating. She countered with red. I said that red meant beets, and beets were good for one thing: throwing out. Since we couldn't agree, we left it to chance. I grabbed Quinn's box of sixty-four Crayola crayons, closed my eyes, and picked.

"What color did you get?"

"Gray." We dined on skim milk.

The color diet book joined the Chun King in the backyard and was replaced by a high-protein diet. Jennifer's not much of a meat eater, so I was surprised.

"You're allowed one glass of wine a day," she explained.

"One glass, or one vase per day?" I asked, noting the King Henry VIII–size goblet she had chosen.

"Dieting is stressful," she said.

"Well, in that case, I'm having a piece of bread."

Whoosh! Out the window went the high-protein diet book. By week's end, the only thing growing in our garden was the pile of diet books.

The first one to fold was Quinn. She might be only three, but it doesn't take a four-year-old to know dieting cuts into one's ice cream allotment.

After putting her to bed with promises of chocolate bars and more cheese than a mouse would want in a lifetime, I came back into the living room. There, in front of the TV, I found Jennifer, miserable, watching the movie *The Mummy*.

"She's so beautiful and so thin," she said of the star, Rachel Weisz.

**By week's end, the only thing growing in our garden was the pile of diet books.**

"You look like her," I said.

"Put your glasses on, Simmons." It was the first time she'd laughed in a week.

"I'm serious." I was, too, and it wasn't just the starvation talking. "I've got the diet for us."

She groaned. "It's called the denial diet," I said. "We pretend we're perfect physical specimens and go on with our lives. You enjoy your wine, and I'll consume all the brown foods I want."

Jennifer liked my idea so much that we celebrated by eating all of Quinn's chocolates. That'll teach her to call us fat.

# Ode to My Puppy #1

Oh dear, what can that odor be,
Oh dear, what can that odor be,
Oh dear, what can that odor be?
Something smells terribly foul.

    Is the toilet backed up?
    Is it sour ketchup?
    Is the garbage pail full
    Of rotting old bull?
    Is it moldy old socks? Sweaty rank jocks?
    Are the nose-plugs fully stocked?

Oh dear, what can that odor be,
Oh dear, what can that odor be,
Oh dear, what can that odor be?
It's only my puppy's breath.

# Lord of the Dance

After about the forty-seventh night in a row of sitting in front of the tube with my wife, watching HGTV, I had a stunning revelation: "I gotta get out of this house!"

Ever since the birth of our daughter, Quinn, Jennifer and I had become housebound. I missed our nights out together. Quinn was old enough now so that we should be able to venture out occasionally. The question was where. I didn't want to go to the theater to watch an Ang Lee film, and hanging around a bar watching the Mets and screaming epithets at the team's owners wasn't tops on her list. Friends had taken dance classes and loved it. The last time I'd danced was years ago in college. And that was on top of a table, gyrating to Blondie.

"Wanna take dance classes?" I asked.

After the initial guffaws, she actually considered it. We're not exactly the dancing type. Jennifer had sworn off anything physical after her days as a high school soccer player when she used to sit on the bench holding the other players' jewelry. But she, too, longed to get out. The problem was that she was busy with a big project at work, and she didn't want to be away from Quinn any more than she had to. We decided I'd stick my toe in the water, and if I liked it, she'd join later.

So, I tippety-tapped my way to Dance New York in Westchester, my local ballroom dance school. I signed up for the beginner's class, a set of five two-hour sessions, where I hoped to come away Phi Beta Kappa in the fox-trot, merengue, swing, and salsa.

As my classmates and I waited to begin, some exchanged work shoes in favor of dance shoes. There was a nod, a quick "hi," but little mingling. We almost seemed embarrassed, we grown-ups, about going back to school.

My class of thirty ranged from recent college grads to card-carrying AARP members. Some could probably trace their ancestry to the Mayflower; for others English was a second language. There were people in good shape and people without a shape. My class consisted mostly of couples, with a few single women. I was the lone unaccompanied male.

"All royt, boys on one side, guhls on the utha!!" That was Clive Phillips. He and his wife, Suzanne, were the owners of the studio and our teachers. Clive, a two-time national ballroom champ, is a lanky Aussie with an easy grin. Suzanne, a gorgeous redhead, was a featured dancer at Radio City Music Hall.

I lined up with the boys on one side, facing the "guhls." It was just like high school but with one big difference— here they *had* to dance with me.

"Let's fox-trot!" yelled Clive. My life as a modern-day Fred Astaire was about to begin! All that was missing was Edward Everett Horton handing me my top hat and tails. Clive demonstrated the basic steps: "Slow, slow, quick-quick."

I was already lost.

He then added a promenade, where you make a V-shape with your partner, then take a couple of forward steps, with an abrupt head-whipping turn to the left thrown in for good measure.

"Now you try," said Clive.

I followed suit, adding a few flourishes along the way: slow, slow, quick-quick-stumble, stumble-stumble, stop, look confused, step, watch, stop, quit.

With the possible exception of listening to an eight-year-old trying to tell a joke, there's nothing more excruciating than watching novices learn a dance. We're awkward, unsure of ourselves, and completely vulnerable.

**I followed suit, adding a few flourishes along the way: slow, slow, quick-quick-stumble, stumble-stumble, stop, look confused, step, watch, stop, quit.**

"Grab a paht-nuh," yelled Clive. Husbands and wives paired off. My partner was Gail, a gum-chewing boomer. I took her hand in mine and placed my right hand on her shoulder. She placed her left hand on my right arm and blew a bubble. It was show time!

"Slow, slow, quick-quick," intoned Clive as we followed his moves.

"You're doing it wrong," said Gail. She corrected the way I held her hand, where my other hand should be on her back, my footwork. I reminded her that as the male, I was the captain of our little ship, and she should follow my lead, even if we were headed straight for an iceberg.

"Fix yer elbow," she said. We'd barely pulled up anchor and already my crew had mutinied and taken over.

"Change paht-nuhs!" Clive and Suzanne have us changing partners frequently so that everyone experiences different styles of dancing (read that to mean "suffers equally").

My next victim was Beth. She greeted me by admitting she had no clue what she was doing. Good! I was free to lead as I saw fit.

"Sorry," I said as I led her into a chair.

"Sorry," I said after I kneed her.

"Sorry," I said as I threw her into another couple.

"Dance is supposed to be fun!" yelled Clive, possibly working off my partner's concerned expression.

"I'm failing dance class," I told Jennifer when I got home. She sympathized for a bit, until Quinn came out to perform. Coincidentally, Quinn had begun dance classes that day, too. She had poise and grace and knew her choreography. A girl who barely graduated to walking two years earlier was doing better than me.

"It's salsa. It's sexy—or it should be!" yelled Clive the following week.

Clive was on an impossible mission to get the rod out of our collective asses. Salsa means "spicy sauce," and as a Latin dance, it's just that. It oozes sensuality. Or at least it's supposed to.

To that end, Clive made us bend our knees, swivel our hips, and punch out the driving beat of the music with the balls of our feet. With our bodies heaving, our necks bobbing, and our legs undulating, we looked like a room full of barfing dogs. To my mind, ours was a group that looked better stiff.

The fact is, at this stage in the dance game, sex is the last thing we beginners are worrying about. We've got a foot fetish going on—and with our own feet. Because that's all we're doing—staring at our feet and wondering why they haven't learned the steps. And yet the sexy stuff will come, Suzanne assured us, especially if we take our eyes off our feet.

It's a simple concept, and when Clive and Suzanne dance, I get it. During one of their biweekly parties, they stepped out on center stage and waltzed. And believe me, it wasn't the waltz that Cinderella and the prince danced. No, no. This was graceful and beautiful and, oh, so sensual. They were more than dance partners; they were lovers.

In watching them, we novices saw the possibilities.

I don't know why I thought I could master ballroom dancing in just a few classes. But it didn't take long to discover it's really hard. I needed a sympathetic ear and knew just who to call.

"I know your pain. I know your pain," says John O'Hurley, after listening to my horror stories. If it weren't for the likes of O'Hurley, the first champ of *Dancing with the Stars*, ballroom dancing would not have become the social monster it is.

"I grew up a little country-club kid in Connecticut, so I had no cultural reference for it." He was talking about the challenge of learning the cha-cha. "My hips had never moved that way."

"But what can I do?" I pleaded. John gave me three tips.

"Ditch the Reebok Classics" was his first. I'd been wearing my favorite sneakers to class, and he didn't approve. "Good dance shoes," he said, "are like a good pair of driving gloves." The shoes are highly flexible, and the suede soles make it easier to glide across the floor.

"Move from the center of your body" was his second suggestion. John bemoaned the fact that most beginners are too busy concentrating on their legs. "Once you learn to relax your legs and move from the core of your abdomen, everything else becomes much simpler."

"What's the third suggestion?"

"Keep a long neck," he said. "It'll give you height, and your body will follow your head." Then he added, "If nothing else, at least it'll make you look like a dancer."

The following class, I did as John had instructed. I bought new shoes—black-and-white jobs that looked like high-end bowling shoes. They made sliding across the floor more pleasant, as I was no longer sticking to it. By concentrating on working from the core of my body, I didn't have quite the herky-jerky movement one gets when relying solely on the legs. And finally, I promenaded around the dance floor with my neck stretched to the limit, as if I were wearing an invisible neck brace. So at least, I hoped, I looked the part. It all helped.

> I promenaded around the dance floor with my neck stretched to the limit, as if I were wearing an invisible neck brace.

"But it wasn't enough," I told Jennifer after she put Mini-Martha Graham to bed. All the other couples were laughing and having fun. My partners had been friendly, forgiving, supportive. But still, "I'm not enjoying it as much as everyone else. Something's missing."

Jennifer spotted the problem. "Want me to take the class with you?"

Jennifer jumped into dance class with gusto. And as expected, she was just as bad as me. She had trouble with her basics, her promenades were anything but, and her turns were merely big veers. Our arms got tangled and our knees knocked. And strangely enough, we were laughing as hard as I could remember. But every so often, we even got a step right. We performed a near-perfect basic and promenade. And we beamed when Suzanne smiled and said, "You got it!"

We left class on a high, to Clive's declaration not to practice at home. "You'll just reinforce all your bad habits," he explained, bucking up my confidence.

At home, I put Quinn to bed, then came out to the living room.

"Let's practice," said Jennifer.

"Clive said we're not supposed to."

"Clive's not here," she said, assuming the dance position.

The fact is, I'll probably never get all the steps down or stop crashing my knees into my partner's legs. But as I danced with Jennifer, I got to laugh with and hold the one person I most wanted to laugh with and hold.

Clive's mantra, to just have fun, finally made sense. I was no longer a slave to my feet. They could do their own damn dance steps as far as I was concerned. If the right wanted to salsa while the left did the swing, so be it. I was now free to hold my wife in my arms—arguably for the first time since our daughter was born and our lives grew so hectic. It was sexy and exhilarating, silly and hilarious. Whether it's the fox-trot, the tango, or the funky chicken— and whether you're in it to raise your energy level or to play Fred and Ginger for one night a week—ultimately, dancing is about having fun.

And I was finally having fun.

# Brush Up on Your Shakespeare

Not long ago, I was watching my nephew play T-ball, and I noticed two things: (a) he sucked at it, and (b) some guy kept shouting at him, "Go back to kickball where you belong!"

My brother, Michael, considered sending his wife over there to punch the loudmouth in the nose, but I talked him out of it. Instead, I insisted he take the high road and insult the man. Looking to the master himself—Billy Shakespeare—for guidance, I suggested to my brother that he paraphrase the Bard and unload on the offender thusly: "Why, you bolting-hutch of beastliness! You swollen parcel of dropsies! You huge bombard of sack! You stuffed cloak-back of guts! You roasted Manningtree ox with the pudding in his belly!!"

The great thing about Shakespearian insults is the insultee isn't sure whether he's been dissed or given a great recipe. By the time ol' Bombard of Sack figured out what he'd been called, the game would be over, and my nephew safe at home playing with his dolls.

> You swollen parcel of dropsies! You huge bombard of sack!

Michael declined the recommendation, however. The lout in question, I was informed, was our father.

# Yankee Doodle Andy

Cannon fire woke me up—that was our alarm clock. It was the first morning of the Battle of Bordentown, New Jersey, and I was with the 5th New York Regiment, Revolutionary War reenactors, preparing to help free my countrymen from the yoke of British oppression yet again.

Dragging myself from the comfort of my Gore-Tex-covered sleeping bag, I slipped on my uniform: flax overalls, a long-sleeve "common shirt," and a fringed hunting shirt over that. I dipped my size-nine feet into a pair of borrowed size-thirteen buckle shoes (my wife gave me pantyhose to stuff in the toes), topped my head with a cocked hat, pulled open the tent flaps, and stumbled into the eighteenth century.

Behind our neat row of white tents, men and women bearing a remarkable resemblance to Paul Revere and Dolley Madison prepared for the day ahead. In the bustling kitchen area, they brewed coffee over a fire they'd built using a flint, a piece of iron, and some charred cloth, while others cleaned muskets and a few tooted on their fifes. Other than overhearing a pair of officers on horseback discussing their colonoscopies, it was my elementary school textbooks come to life.

A few hours later, the cannons roared again—this time they were pointed at the enemy. The first battle had begun, and our objective was to hold the field, the one across the street from the Ocean Spray plant. Altogether, there were about five hundred on our side versus four hundred Brits, Loyalists, and Hessians, all under the watchful eye of a thousand spectators.

"Shoulder firelock!" came the order from our first sergeant, John Cronin, a soft-spoken police officer from Fishkill, New York. "Make ready . . . Take aim . . . Fire!"

The 5th New York's muskets came alive. We were only using black powder, no musket balls, but since I was a newbie, I couldn't even be trusted with that.

"You might accidentally triple-pack the barrel and blow yourself up," I was told. Instead, I had to settle for yelling, "Bang!" But even with a ferocious "bang!" the Brits kept advancing.

"That's the problem with the Brits," said Sean, one of the guys in my unit. "They never want to die."

"It's the uniforms," I suggested. "They don't want to dirty them."

"No," said Jimmy, to my left, "it's because they drove three hours to get here and no one wants to die too fast."

"Close up the ranks!" ordered Cronin. "Shoulder firelock! Andy, other shoulder! Fix bayonet! Take aim! Andy, don't point your musket at Ed's head!"

We fired off another volley. *Boom! Boom! Boom!* BANG! *Boom!*

Joe Ryan, our larger-than-life captain, ordered, "CHARGE BAYONET!" Then, rearing back his six-foot-five body, he let loose, "HUZZAH!"

"Huzzah!" we bellowed back. "Huzzah! Huzzah! Huzzah!"

The Brits gave us everything they had—muskets, cannons . . . But if they weren't dying, neither were we. Nimbly sidestepping volley after volley, we took the day.

Nothing like a bunch of crazed reenactors charging with fixed bayonets and huzzahing their lungs out to get the Brits to fall.

\* \* \*

"YOU WON'T BE A VIRGIN AFTER TOMORROW!" said Joe, speaking in capital letters like he always did. It was a few hours after the battle, and we were sitting around the tents enjoying some period-appropriate booze. He handed me a box of paper cartridges loaded with black powder. "YOU'RE GOING TO FIRE YOUR MUSKET," he said.

The next day, after forcing them from their redoubts, the 5th New York and the Continental Line army found themselves facing off against King George III's men and their allies. It was now time to load my Brown Bess musket.

I removed a paper cartridge from the box, bit off the tip, shook a little black powder into the musket's "pan," shut the pan, poured the rest down the barrel, and shouldered my musket.

"Make ready . . ." I took the musket off my shoulder and cocked the hammer all the way back. "Take aim . . ." I stared down the barrel at the Redcoats. "Fire!" I pulled the trigger and the flint smashed into the frizzen, causing a spark that ignited the black powder, which went boom!

Joe grinned. "PRETTY COOL, HUH?!"

Before I could respond, "You're damn right," an officer ran through our ranks yelling, "Take casualties!" We'd won yesterday, so today it was the Redcoats' turn. Since there was no actual Battle of Bordentown, we could wage war however we wanted.

"THIS IS IT, BOYS," said Joe. "WE'RE ALL GOING DOWN. FIX BAYONETS!"

The Scottish Highlanders responded by firing off a volley. Troops around us fell. In a single motion, one body hit the ground, rolled over, and produced a cell phone with which he began snapping photos.

"CHARGE!" yelled Joe.

"Huzzah! Huzzah! Huzzah!" we yelled.

One by one we went down, until it was my turn. Reenactment, I'd been told, is part theater. So, with that in mind, I channeled Sonny Corleone getting it at the tollbooth. The result: My gyrating death throes had the graceful choreography of squirrels throwing a party in my pants. And then I died, denting my canteen in the process.

> My gyrating death throes had the graceful choreography of squirrels throwing a party in my pants.

The Scots charged over us, pushing the rest of our line into the woods. It was what we did to them yesterday, only we suffered the added ignominy of having to look up their kilts.

"By the order of the ghost of King George III," announced a British officer, "all rise from the dead."

We stood up to a hearty round of applause. Even the Brits were impressed. "Good dying," one said.

As militias from both sides laughed and embraced, I recalled what another reenactor, Mitch Lee, told me: "This is not a hobby. This is a lifestyle."

Huzzah!!

# Ode to My Puppy #2

Oh, little puppy, oh, little puppy,
Why do you eat so much?
You ate the turkey, the ham, the steak, and such,
The ribs, the trout, the pie without fuss.
The lettuce, the tomatoes, the potatoes, and more,
The pillows, the sneakers, and couches galore.
Oh, little puppy, oh, little puppy,
Why do you eat so much?
Oh, little puppy, oh, little puppy,
Now you have thrown-uppy.

# Making Up Is Hard to Do

**The fight began while I was massaging my wife's feet.**

We were curled up on the couch. I was kneading and caressing Jennifer's insole and heel. Each little piggy was carefully attended to, as was every corn, callus, and bunion. Then, into the third hour, I got to thinking, *Wouldn't it be great if someone else were doing this?* Only I didn't think it—I said it.

There was silence from the east end of the sofa. I sped up the massage and suggested we switch on HGTV. "They're remodeling bathrooms!" I said, a little too eager to please.

Too late. "I don't ask you for much," she said, moving to the easy chair. "May I please have the remote?" She was angry. I could tell because Jennifer gets polite when she's angry. And then the fight was on. I knew because we weren't saying anything. When we're not fighting, Jennifer can wax eloquent on any subject. While watching *Ghost Whisperer* last month, she held forth on the topic "Is it me, or does Jennifer Love Hewitt's haircut look off?"

Well, two can play this game—I buried my nose in the *New York Times* crossword puzzle. Since it was a Thursday, I got only three clues right. But there I sat, staring at twenty-seven down (Beverly Sills's shoe size), pointedly ignoring Jennifer and the couples remodeling their hampers.

Jennifer was the first to cave. It was a few hours later. The local news was now on, and I had just figured out that Beverly Sills wore a size "bix" when Jennifer whispered, "I'm sorry." She's not a fighter, and the pressure was killing her. She sat on my lap and kissed me ever so tenderly, just as sports came on.

Frankly, I see no reason why I can't kiss my wife and watch Mets highlights simultaneously. However, this seems to break fight-makeup protocol, in which it is spelled out in some handbook (which I apparently misplaced) that when your wife wants to bury the hatchet, you are not allowed to watch sports.

"You don't want to kiss me?"

"I do. But I would prefer to kiss you during the weather."

Off my lap and back to the chair she went.

"All night I watched couples agonize over the benefits of the Centerset Double Handle Lavatory Faucet from the Victorian Collection versus the Widespread High-Arc Lavatory Faucet," I reminded her. "But when sports comes on . . ."

"May I please have the remote?"

If she thinks she can take that tone with me . . .

Earlier, Jennifer had pointed out that she doesn't ask me for much. And it's true. I'm the needy one. The one who must have his jokes laughed at, who needs his hand held when we go to parties, the one who asks when we go out for dinner, "Can I get dessert?"

"C'mon, I'll massage your feet," I offered. Before I knew it, she was on the couch and her calloused, bunioned, corned feet on my lap. If only I knew Braille—what a story those feet could tell.

Now it was her turn. She switched on ESPN. And as the Mets scored the go-ahead run . . .

> If only I knew Braille—what a story those feet could tell.

"So," she said, "do you think Jennifer Love Hewitt will grow out her hair?"

# "In Five Hundred Feet, You Will Be Lost"

"Men," goes the old chestnut, "will drive to Minsk before stopping to ask for directions to the corner store." Not me.

I'll burn branches in the form of SOS on the hood of my car rather than navigate my way out of being lost. And lost in a car is where you'll usually find me. See, I have this problem: If I ask someone for directions and the response is longer than, "It's over there," I zone out.

Case in point, on a family trip last year I stopped and asked a gentleman for directions. As we drove away, I turned to my wife, Jennifer. "Did you notice his teeth?"

"You didn't listen to a word he said, did you?" she asked.

"Not a one. I was looking at his teeth. Both of them were yellow—curry color, actually. More Thai than Indian . . ."

"So we're still lost."

"Yes."

Well, my wandering days are over, for I am now the proud owner of a TomTom One Global Positioning System!

"A what?" asked Jennifer.

"A GPS, a NAV, a little thingy that uses satellites to get us from point A to point B without having to stop and ask strangers."

Jennifer doubted I could master such a complex piece of machinery. "You can't even get the time stamp off our photos," I was reminded. It's true. Every photo we take is dated February 12, 1983 (the year, it so happens, that camera manufacturers figured out how to put the red dot in everyone's eyes). Now obviously I'm not the first person to use a GPS. They've been around a few years. But this was a pretty big leap for me, a charter member of the Rand McNally fan club.

It's not that I'm a technological ignoramus, as the guys in IT insist. I'm a "tech-no," which means I'm a technological ignoramus by choice. But I don't want to become an anachronism, so I vowed to kick the tires on some new technology.

The first thing I did was buy a Spinbrush for my teeth. I then downloaded songs onto an iPod. (Have you heard of these things? You input music into them, then spend the rest of the day trying to keep the earbuds from falling out of your ear.) Now it was on to the GPS. If I'm going to get lost, I want to be able to blame it on an expensive piece of machinery.

TomTom came fully loaded: route planning, traffic and weather alerts, and an optional warning when I'm exceeding the speed limit. I declined the last feature, as my car was already equipped with that feature. It's called Jennifer.

> **If I'm going to get lost, I want to be able to blame it on an expensive piece of machinery.**

TomTom also let me choose a celebrity voice to give me directions. I passed on John Cleese because when you've made a wrong turn, the last thing you want is to be berated by your navigational system. It struck me as odd—not to mention dangerous—to be taking driving tips from Gary Busey, so I nixed him. The same went for Mr. T. Listening to him say, "I pity the fool who doesn't take the next left," for two hours would have resulted in my driving over a cliff.

Of the nonceleb voices, Sylvie had a come-hither-to-yon-destination bedroom voice, while Mandy's bland, nonconfrontational demeanor reminded us of everyone's second-favorite aunt. We went with Mandy.

We were now prepared to put TomTom to the test on a trip that would take us from Jennifer's mother's home in Rochester, New York, to my sister's in Ithaca—two hours and six minutes away. I tapped in the coordinates (a fancy term for addresses) on the NAV's touch screen, which—since I was able to do it—means it was pretty easy. Seeing the colorful screen come alive, our four-year-old, Quinn, assumed it was a small TV. "Hannah Montana!" she shouted.

"No, upstate New York," I corrected. With bags packed and car humming, we put our trip in Mandy's hands.

At the first intersection, Mandy promptly intoned, "Turn right."

"Aren't we supposed to turn left?" Jennifer asked.

We were already lost. We'd made this trip dozens of times, and this was not our normal route.

"Maybe she knows a better way," I said, making the right turn.

"In a quarter-mile, turn left. . . . In one hundred twenty-five yards, turn left," said Mandy. "Turn left."

Maybe because Mandy's not much of a conversationalist, Quinn put in another request for *Hannah Montana*.

"Do you know where we're going?" asked Jennifer.

"Not a clue, but it's pretty," I said.

Mandy, it appears, is a bit of a sightseer. Rather than have us take 390 to 90, as I had assumed, she had us toodling through bucolic Pittsford. It then dawned on me that when I input my preferences, I'd opted for the cheapskate route, skipping all tolls, something we'd never done before. Mandy was saving me money. If we could just skip 372 more tolls, she would pay for herself. I was fully prepared to forget all about the coquettish Sylvie when Mandy grew quiet. Too quiet.

"I think that's a flaw," said Jennifer. "Mandy should be making encouraging remarks all along, just to assure us that she's still on the job. Things like 'You're on the right track' and 'You're an excellent driver.'"

"In half a mile, turn right." Mandy was back in the game!

"In one hundred twenty-five yards, turn right. . . . In fifty yards, turn right. . . . Turn right."

I turned left. I am sometimes susceptible to the same Right Shoe, Left Foot syndrome Quinn suffers from, and in this instance, I put on my left shoe when I needed my right. Mandy was confused. She didn't know where we were and had to ad-lib.

"I've never heard a computer say 'Uhhh . . .' before," said Jennifer.

"Let Mandy get her bearings."

"Hannah Montana!"

"Turn left, then right," said Mandy with a forcefulness we'd not known.

> "I've never heard a computer say 'Uhhh . . .' before."

"Take the second left." I did exactly as I was told and turned into a Home Depot parking lot.

What she'd meant was the left after Home Depot. This seems to be a growing problem—idiots like me taking our directives literally. In Germany, a man followed the command "turn right now" thirty yards before the intended junction. He drove his four-by-four onto a building site, up a stairway, and into a Porta-Potty. Another guy plowed into a pile of sand on a highway after trusting his GPS more than a Closed for Construction sign.

Getting out of Home Depot was hungry work, so I tapped the NAV's screen until I got to a cool feature—Points of Interest. Some taps later and, voilà, a list of restaurants in the area appeared. You can also find gas stations, hotels, even a hospital, which was good, since while I was punching away at the tiny keyboard, I almost punched us into the back of a Toyota parked at a red light.

The jury is out on just how safe GPS devices are—there are no major studies proving one way or the other. But common sense suggests that Mandy telling me where to go saves me from fumbling with cumbersome maps. On the other hand, human nature being what it is, why watch the road when I can watch my progress on the small, colorful screen, or surf the NAV for the area's best French cruller?

Other systems offer voice recognition, which means you don't have to tap anything. Simply say in a loud, clear voice, "Find cruller," then Mandy tells you how to get there.

"You have reached your destination," said Mandy, sounding relieved as we pulled into my sister's driveway. It took us two hours and thirteen minutes, seven minutes longer than if we'd taken the toll routes.

Frankly, a map would've also gotten us to Ithaca, and for $495 less. But I did appreciate how Mandy took charge when I got lost, and who knows, maybe in the future we'll use a GPS for everything. Like finding that golf ball I launched into the forest, showing me how to bypass the scented-soaps aisle in the supermarket, or pointing out to this dim father just who Hannah Montana is.

# "Plutonic" Friends

It was bedlam in the formerly tranquil Simmons household. Voices were raised, fists pounded tables, Mr. Potato Head was torn asunder.

I could see it on the evening news—our neighbor Mrs. Stein telling the world, "But they were such a nice family, even if they didn't always mow their lawn, or remember what day to put out the garbage, or . . ."

What was the to-do about? What could stir such animosity?

"Pluto is too a planet!" yelled Jennifer.

"Is not!" I bellowed back.

Jennifer poured a glass of wine and stood by the window, staring defiantly into the night sky at Pluto. I didn't have the heart to tell her she was gazing at a streetlamp.

"The International Astronomical Union is the sole authority for classifying, naming, and making things up about outer space," I reminded her as I squished into our new wing chair. "These are very smart people, smart enough to figure out how to make a living from going to Star Trek conventions. So if they think that, after seventy-six years of placing the word *planet* on its business card, Pluto is only an icy rock playing dress-up, then case closed."

Jennifer wasn't buying into what she considered an arbitrary new rule: that a planet isn't just something that's round and orbits the sun—it must also be big enough and have enough gravitational force to "clear its area" of any similar-sized objects.

"If that's the case, your aunt Ruth could be a planet," she sputtered. "She's round, cold, and she cleared her area of everything long ago, including your uncle Danny, who ran off with the dog walker."

Hearing that Pluto was planet non grata, our three-year-old, Quinn, removed the Pluto action figure from her Disney display. It made Jennifer even sadder.

"I wonder, if it had a more serious name, say Sidney or Desmond, might its fate have been different?" Jennifer asked aloud.

"Look," I said, shifting my weight around on the chair, hoping circulation would return to my legs. "As the sole authority for classifying, naming, and making things up about our home, let's use Pluto's demotion to make a few changes around here, starting with this wing chair."

"My grandmother left me that."

"Sorry, but this does not fit the new definition of a chair."

"What new definition?"

"The one I'm making up as I speak. From here on out, a chair isn't just something that someone sits on. Otherwise, I'd be a chair if Quinn had her way. In my dictionary, a chair is something you want to sit on, preferably in front of a TV. It also needs to be ratty enough to chase everyone but me from its orbit. *That's* a chair. Oh, and my father's penchant for leaving diners with his pockets full of Sweet'N Low? That's now shopping, and not—as your family refers to it—stealing."

Through the window, I could see Quinn walking in the yard, holding a bag of okra.

"Bravo!" I shouted as I jumped to my feet. Quinn had redefined okra as a garden tool to be stored in the outdoor shed, thus guaranteeing that neither Jennifer nor I would ever find it and cook it for dinner.

Jennifer was still upset. And when she stews, all of her 83,543,291,732 brain cells are put on time and a half.

"Should we get rid of Quinn because she's the shortest and hasn't learned to clear her Polly Pocket dolls from her orbit or ours?" she asked. "What does this mean for anything that doesn't quite fit the mold? What does this mean for Rhode Island? For doughnut holes? For Danny DeVito?"

> Quinn had redefined okra as a garden tool to be stored in the outdoor shed.

Jennifer was looking at the larger picture, larger than the universe. "What does it say about a galaxy that changes the rules for convenience's sake?"

I didn't have an answer, other than to say, "Hey, wanna watch TV?"

In the end, Jennifer, Quinn, and I were one happy planet, seated on our uncomfortable wing chair, our eyes orbiting *The Biggest Loser*. If little Pluto was in need of loving, it would find it in this household.

But for its own comfort, tell it to bring a chair.

# How to Ruin a Joke

A classic joke goes like this: A nurse rushes into an exam room and says, "Doctor, doctor, there's an invisible man in the waiting room." The doctor says, "Tell him I can't see him."

Pretty simple, right?

Here's how I tell it: "A nurse—her name is Joyce—feels a presence in the waiting room. She looks around but sees nothing. She jumps up from her desk, carefully replaces her chair, and runs down the lavender-hued hallway to the doctor's office. She knocks on the door. No response. He's not there. Where can he be? She continues down the hall, admiring a lithograph of an eighteenth-century Mississippi paddleboat along the way." By this time, my audience has left, but I soldier on. "She bursts into the exam room and says, 'Doctor, doctor!' The doctor, I should mention, is a urologist with a degree from Ohio State, which is where my nephew . . ."

You get the idea. I'm an embellisher. I can't leave a simple gag alone.

I'm not the only joke-challenged member of the family. My sister's worse than I am. Her problem: She can't remember them. "A nurse rushes into an exam room and says . . . Uh, let me start all over again. A nurse rushes into a waiting . . . No, it's not the waiting room. She just came from the waiting room. Let me start all over again. A doctor rushes into . . . No, wait . . ."

My grandfather's different. He's guilty of taking a perfectly fine joke and selling it as the second coming of Oscar Wilde: "Okay, this is a good one. Ready? No, really, ready?

Okay, fasten your seat belts. Ready? A nurse . . . Got it? A nurse? Okay, ready? A nurse rushes into an exam room and says, 'Doctor, doctor, there's an invisible man in the waiting room.' Now, this is where it gets funny. Ready?"

No one is ever ready, so they leave before he gets to the punch line.

My uncle is on Wall Street, so he hears all the jokes before they hit the web. And he lets you know he knows them all by telling you all of them. He also knows that most people don't like jokes. So he slips them in under the radar: "I was chatting with Ben Bernanke the other day. You know Ben, don't you? The Fed chief? Anyhoo, we were reviewing the Fed's policy on long-term interest rates, and he told me it had evolved into its current iteration only after a nurse rushed into an exam room and said, 'Doctor, doctor, there's . . .' Hey, where are you going?"

My brother Mark understands that the secret to good joke-telling is to know your audience. When he entertained my grandmother's mah-jongg club one evening, he made it a point to adapt the joke to them: "A stacked nurse rushes into an exam room . . ."

No one in my family has ever finished this joke.

But as bad as it is not to be able to tell a joke, there's something worse: not being able to listen to one. Take my cousin Mitch.

"Why couldn't the doctor see him?" he asked.

"Because he's invisible," I said.

## No one in my family has ever finished this joke.

"Now, I didn't get that. I thought the doctor couldn't see him because he was with a patient."

"Well, yeah, okay, but the fact that the guy was invisible . . ."

"Could the nurse see him?"

"No. She's the one who said he was invisible . . ."

"How'd she know he was there?"

"Because he . . ."

"When you say he was invisible, does that mean his clothes were invisible, too?"

Here's where I tried to walk away.

"Because if his clothes weren't invisible," Mitch said, stepping between me and the exit, "then the doctor could see him, right?"

"Yeah, but . . ."

"At least his clothes."

"I guess . . ."

"Unless he was naked."

"Okay, he was naked!"

"Why would he go to his doctor naked?"

Next time you see my family and someone's telling a joke, do yourself a favor: Make yourself invisible.

# Itching for a Fight

I've suddenly become nostalgic for my old one-room, half-bath, twelve-story walk-up in the city's hovel district. Let me explain.

It all started simply enough. Soon after we moved to the country, Jennifer decided that our backyard was sorely in need of some landscaping work.

"What's wrong with it?" I asked. "Look at how fat and sassy our grass is. I bet we have the fattest, sassiest lawn in the neighborhood."

That's when Jennifer let me in on a little secret. There is no grass on our lawn. Only fat, sassy poison ivy.

I pointed out that, unlike everything else in the yard, the ivy was thriving and maybe we should go after something else, like that malingering rosebush.

"Why evict the one thing that actually wants to be here?" I reasoned.

Here's why: Jennifer doesn't like poison ivy. Something about the word poison makes her think it can't be good for you.

So we called in landscapers to get estimates. The first took one look at our lawn, then called his car dealer and ordered a BMW, the one that comes with a chauffeur. The second charged by the blade of grass. That's when I drove into town looking for one of those cheap illegal aliens the media insists is on every street corner in America.

"Are you an illegal alien?" I asked the first man I saw.

"No, I'm the mayor," he said.

"Are you an illegal alien?" I asked another.

"No, I'm your neighbor."

"Are you an illegal alien?"

"No, I'm your wife, you idiot," said Jennifer, shoving a rake in my hand and telling me to take care of things myself.

One of the problems with poison ivy is you can't simply grab it by the collar and toss it out like some drunk from a bar. You have to suit up for battle—rubber gloves duct-taped to a long-sleeved shirt buttoned to your neck. Long pants with the cuffs duct-taped over your socks and work boots. A scarf wrapped tightly around your neck and face, duct-taped to goggles and a hat, completes the jackass look. Armed with a pruner and some weed killer, I was no longer simply a homeowner unable to find an illegal alien to do the work he didn't want to do. I was, in fact, a Knight of the Backyard Realm.

Since I had no idea what poison ivy looked like, I kept my plan of attack simple: Anything remotely planty goes. Ferns? Gone! Hosta? Gone! Rosebush? Gone! Trees? Gone! Mailbox? Gone! I was Sherman marching on Atlanta, laying waste to anything in my path. What the weed killer didn't get, I ripped out by hand. What I couldn't rip out, I ran over with my car.

"That's the Japanese maple!" screamed Jennifer.

"Now it's mulch," I said, grinning devilishly over the whirring engine of my '95 Oldsmobile Cutlass Supreme.

By the end of the day, I'd rid the yard of all the poison ivy, save for one sorry little clump. Like the heads of the vanquished left on spikes outside medieval castle walls, it served as a warning to any of its kin that might dare to show their shiny leaves around here.

Hot and tired and feeling pretty damn good about myself, I unraveled the four rolls of duct tape that had adhered to my body and stepped out of my sweat-soaked clothes—twenty-seven pounds lighter than when I entered them. The shrieks of horror from my seventy-eight-year-old neighbor spying my naked body startled me so much that I tripped down a small embankment, only to be saved by the soft, pillowy embrace of the remaining clump of poison ivy.

As I bathed in calamine lotion, Jennifer figured out that all my tireless work had reduced our home's value by a third. So she hired one of the landscapers to return the yard to its previous state of disrepair. We went with the guy who charged by the blade of grass. With no lawn left, how expensive could he be?

> Since I had no idea what poison ivy looked like, I kept my plan of attack simple: Anything remotely planty goes.

# Buff Your Shoes with a Banana

My parents dropped by to help with a project I'd put off: cleaning the house. Now, Mom and Dad are—hmm, how do I put this delicately?—cheap!

So when I offered to pick up cleaning supplies, they said, "Never mind. You have everything we need right here in the house. Where's the vinegar?"

"Here," I said, bringing out the twelve-year-old balsamic. Mom pushed past me and found the distilled white vinegar. She instructed me to make a sandwich and get out of her way.

As I ate my ham on white, I watched her tackle a carpet stain with the vinegar. I thought it a bit odd, but less so than her sniffing my bookshelf. When one book caused her nose to wrinkle, she walked it over to the kitchen and deposited it into the freezer.

"That'll get rid of that stale odor for a while," she said. I nodded in agreement, although I wasn't sure what I was agreeing to. "Hey, there's broken glass here. Did you do it?"

I shrugged. Grabbing the sandwich out of my hand, Mom threw the ham to the dog, wiped the mayo across my scalp, and carefully mopped up the glass shards with the fresh bread.

"Hey!" I protested.

"Mayonnaise is a hair conditioner," she said. "And picking up tiny slivers of glass is easy with white bread."

Mom had lost her marbles, and I thought it only fitting that her husband should know. I found Dad in the yard, mixing an ounce of vodka, some liquid dish soap, and two cups of water in a spray bottle.

"I'm hunting weeds," he said, seeing my puzzled expression.

"With vodka?"

"Apply this mixture on a sunny day." Spritz. "It won't kill the weeds." Spritz. "But the alcohol does dry 'em up." Spritz, spritz.

"You do realize that's the Grey Goose?" He didn't care.

Is everyone crazy? I thought as I walked back into the house, where Mom was buffing my shoes with banana peels.

"Mom, what are you . . ." BAM! I slipped on a banana peel. "Ooh, my back . . ."

**"You do realize that's the Grey Goose?" He didn't care.**

"Don't move," she yelled. "I'll get the meat tenderizer!"

But first she pulled off my shoe, grabbed a sock, and disappeared into the kitchen. I tried to run for my life, but Mom was quick. She returned with a paste made from meat tenderizer and water, and rubbed it on the small of my back. She then placed my sock, which she'd filled with dried kidney beans and microwaved for thirty seconds, over the paste.

Before I had a chance to call 911, a curious thing happened—my back began to feel better! The enzymes in the meat tenderizer were soothing my aching muscles. And the beanbag sock worked like a heating pad.

Suddenly, I saw things anew. My shoes were clean. And though the carpet smelled like salad dressing, the stain was gone. Out in the yard stood Dad, sipping his weed killer and admiring his handiwork: shriveled weeds.

As crazy as it sounds, my parents were right. We don't always have to buy specialized cleaners or expensive, chemical-filled concoctions. We already own many of the things we need to clean a house, mend a household item, or soothe a bruised back.

To celebrate my clean house, I invited them to stay for dinner. They declined. They had company coming over and had to make a big salad.

"First," said Mom, "I have to throw the lettuce into the washing machine."

Huh?*

_____

*Place a pillowcase inside another, fill with rinsed lettuce leaves, tie both pillowcases with string, and throw into the washing machine with a towel for balance. Run the spin cycle, and you've turned your washer into a giant salad spinner.

# How Sweet It Is

**"What are you doing?"**
**"I'm reading the menu."**
**"No, with your hand," I said.**

"I'm holding the menu," my father said defensively.

"With the *other* hand."

We were seated at a booth in a diner. Dad was hiding something in that paw, which he stealthily slid across the tabletop before stuffing it into his pocket.

"You're stealing Sweet'N Low, aren't you?'

"It's not stealing; they want you to take it. That's why they leave it out here."

"They leave it out here for you to put in the coffee that they serve you."

"How else am I expected to get Sweet'N Low for my coffee at home?"

"Dad, I know you don't get around as much anymore. But let me clue you into something: They have these things called supermarkets. And inside these stores are aisles. And in the aisles are shelves. Lots of shelves filled with goods. And next to the sugar . . ."

"Everybody does it."

"I don't."

"And you never have Sweet'N Low in your house. Next time I come over I'd appreciate it if you stopped by a coffee shop and picked up a few packets."

"If it's not stealing, then why are you sneaking them? Why not go from table to table stuffing all the Sweet'N Low packets into your pockets?"

"Because those customers wouldn't have any to take home with them."

Dad was a remarkably ethical criminal. I'd recently read an article about a thief who, after robbing a home, cleaned the house and even did the dishes. If Dad took to breaking and entering, I'd like to think he'd do the same.

"He saw me," he said. Dad's fingers were in the sweetener bowl when he noticed the manager eyeballing him. "Quick, take the Sweet'N Low." He shoved seven packets of pink gold my way.

"Why don't you just put the Sweet'N Low back?"

"And admit I'm wrong?"

"You *are* wrong!"

"Can I help you, gentlemen?" asked the manager. I ripped open the seven packets of Sweet'N Low and dumped the contents into my half-empty coffee cup and took a sip. All that was missing was some perfume dripped into my eyes and I would have had the full lab-rat experience.

"Yeah, two more cups," said Dad, cool as a cucumber. The manager spotted the empty sweetener bowl. Dad smiled. The man smiled back, then took a full bowl from another table and placed it on ours before leaving. Dad quickly emptied the contents into his pockets.

> All that was missing was some perfume dripped into my eyes and I would have had the full lab-rat experience.

I'm not sure why he steals Sweet'N Low. I think it's because Dad comes from a long line of petty thieves who looked upon restaurants and supermarkets as bargain-basement dollar stores. On those rare occasions his mother dined out, it was to stock up on provisions. She'd bring along a handbag large enough to store bread, pats of butter, salt and pepper shakers, any silverware she might be short on at the time, and the occasional salad plate. One of his aunts thought nothing of strolling around the supermarket snacking on grapes and cherries before settling down for lunch at the olive bar.

Dad rifled through the bowl again, making sure he hadn't missed anything worth filching. He won't take the yellow or blue. He's loyal to his brand.

It's funny, other than his long-time love for Sweet'N Low, there isn't one specific thing that I really remember about my father growing up. He had a good sense of humor. He was always around. He never spanked me. Hell, I can't recall him ever really yelling at me, except maybe when I deserved it. And even then it was drudgery for him. But that one thing?

Friends of mine have fond memories of an incredible trip to the Grand Canyon that their fathers took them on, or the ski trip to Vail. We never did any of that. Dad was a true son of Brooklyn, before the hipsters took over. And as tough as he was, the Grand Canyon had snakes and soil, and he wanted no part of any of that. As for skiing, why be cold when you could stay inside a nice, warm apartment in New York? Our vacations, when we took them, were usually spent near a racetrack or up at the Holiday Inn in Tarrytown, about forty minutes from home. It had a pool and it had . . . a pool. What else did we need? Plus there was a basketball hoop and a field big enough to toss a ball.

We were a formidable two-on-two basketball team, Dad and I. I'd feed him the ball, and he'd take it to the hoop. In football, it was reversed. He was the quarterback, a south-paw whose delivery confounded everyone. I was the fleet-footed receiver who longed to be on the other end of one of his perfect passes.

We were complementary teammates, and teammates we would remain, even when I got older.

On a visit home from college, my dog had gotten sick all over the white living-room rug—my mother's pride and joy. I was furiously cleaning it up when Dad happened by. "What are you doing?" he said, blissfully unaware of the horror to come.

"Phineas crapped all over the rug!" I whispered anxiously.

His smile disappeared, and his mouth formed a large oval shape as he placed both hands on his cheeks. Depending on your reference point, he was either *The Scream* or Macaulay Culkin in *Home Alone*. He then looked furtively around. "I'll distract your mother," he said, before running off into the other room.

Dad had my back, always. That I do remember. No matter what I said, or what idiocy I engaged in, I was protected.

"Here you are, gentlemen." The manager placed two new cups of coffee down in front of us and turned to leave.

"Excuse me," I said, freezing him. I held up the bowl of sweeteners. "There are no Sweet'N Lows. Mind getting us some?"

# The Dow of Pooh

My daughter's favorite bedtime stories have always included Winnie the Pooh. Whether these adventures came from the nimble mind of A. A. Milne or something I was forced to concoct on those days we traveled and left her book at home, Pooh, Tigger, Roo, and the other denizens of the Hundred Acre Wood had to see her off to slumberland.

And though she's reached the grand old age of nine, Quinn still enjoys a good Pooh tale. With apologies to Mr. Milne, here's one I dreamed up recently during the waning days of the Great Recession. In this story, it is revealed that one of the great stock-market shamans isn't Warren Buffet or even Jim Cramer, but is, in fact, none other than the consummately calm, reflective bear—Winnie the Pooh.

While Eeyore frets, "Zynga or Genentech?"

And Piglet hesitates, "If I wait, the price of the stock will surely fall."

Pooh simply is, "I'll just buy a mutual fund."

## In Which Pooh Learns How Companies Raise the Value of Their Stock

*Pooh and Rabbit have gone into business together making and selling Cottleston pies. Much to their surprise and pleasure, the business has done quite well.*

"Hallo, Rabbit," said Pooh, entering Rabbit's office.

"I'm a chief executive officer, Pooh. Please address me as 'Mr. Rabbit,'" Rabbit chided.

"Hallo, Mr. Rabbit," said Pooh.

"Hello, Pooh," said Rabbit. "These reports you gave me show production and profits soaring! We've actually sold three pies! If this keeps up, I predict our stock will rise forty-two percent. And by year's end we will have sold *five* pies!"

"Maybe we shall build new Cottleston pie factories and hire hundreds of chefs and make more Cottleston pies," said Pooh, dreaming of a world full of Cottleston pies.

"I've a better idea. I'm laying off workers," declared Rabbit.

"But . . ." said a confused Pooh.

"Wall Street loves unemployment," explained Rabbit. "In fact, I'll hire Roo, Kanga, and Tigger just so I can fire them."

This was much too much for a Bear of Very Little Brain.

"Laying off workers lets everyone know our operation is efficient," said Rabbit.

"How many workers are you planning to let go?" asked Pooh.

"The entire workforce," answered Rabbit.

Pooh tried to figure out how many workers would be left if the entire workforce were laid off.

"And this is just the beginning," said Rabbit, proving his point that it was, in fact, just the beginning by moving on to the middle. "We'll expand! We'll buy other corporations, then close them down as well."

There was something nagging at Pooh, but he couldn't think what it was. Oh, yes . . .

"But who will produce the Cottleston pies?" For a Pooh, this was a most important question.

"Who cares about Cottleston pies! We're improving efficiency. By the way, I'll have to lay you off, too. I'm sorry, Pooh. You're a nice bear and have done a great job, even if I did have to keep reminding you not to taste every single pie that came out of the oven."

"But I'm the chief funancial officer," said Pooh.

"That's chief *fin*ancial officer, Pooh," corrected Rabbit. "And frankly, having a chief financial officer when there are no finances to preside over isn't efficient. Once I've announced that you've been laid off, I expect the company's stock to double. Then I'll fire myself, dissolve the company, and the stock will go through the roof!"

"But then there's no company," said Pooh, still confused by modern economic theory.

"Perfect! A nonexisting company is the model

> "Then I'll fire myself, dissolve the company, and the stock will go through the roof!"

of efficiency. No overtime, no benefits to be paid out, no overhead! If every corporation laid off all their workers and shut their doors, America would be much better off. We could compete with anyone, anywhere!"

Rabbit stopped. He had just thought of something troublesome.

"Hmm . . . of course, my new wealth will send me into a higher tax bracket."

"What tax racquet are you in now?" asked Pooh.

"The zero-percent tax bracket. I'll have to take deductions. I know—I shall donate my body to a taxidermy school."

"What shall I do?" asked Pooh.

"If I were you," advised Rabbit, "I would start buying stock in the company."

## In Which Tigger Exudes Irrational Exuberance

*With interest rates at all-time lows, Tigger convinces Piglet to cash out his safe bond and income mutual funds and go where the real money is: day-trading. Piglet is quite nervous. After all, it is hard to be an aggressive stock trader when you are only a Very Small Animal.*

"Tiggers like this Microwiz stock best of all," said Tigger as he bounced on the buy button of his computer.

"Then I shall buy Microwiz, too," said Piglet. "Now, let us look for Pooh, who . . ."

"SELL! SELL! SELL! Tiggers don't like Microwiz stock!" exclaimed Tigger, bouncing on the sell button.

"But I thought Tiggers liked Microwiz stock best of all," said a confused Piglet.

"No, Tiggers like *Macro*wiz stocks best of all. BUY! BUY! BUY!" said Tigger, while purchasing stock in Macrowiz.

So Piglet did what Piglets do, which is to do what they're told. He sold Microwiz at a loss and bought Macrowiz. "Now, Pooh must surely be . . ."

"SELL! SELL! SELL!" blurted Tigger as he bounced all about the room, clear out the window and back in through another window. "SELL! SELL! SELL!!!! Tiggers don't like Macrowiz."

"But Tigger, I thought Tiggers liked Macrowiz best of all?"

"Tiggers like *Mid*wiz best of all!" And so Piglet bought Midwiz.

*By the end of one day as a day trader, Piglet is frazzled, broke, and drunk on acorn wine. Piglets, one should be warned, are nasty drunks—like many Very Small Animals. Poor Roo discovered this when a besotted Piglet yelled at* him to "leave my damn lawn and go play where the Woozle wasn't!"

## In Which Christopher Robin and Pooh Come to an Enchanted Place and Pooh Leaves a Small Present Before Saying Good-Bye

After witnessing the effect the stock market had on his friends, Pooh wished to pay a visit. So he packed up his small fortune (his seventeen pots of golden, delicious honey) then he and Christopher Robin left the forest and ventured to the New York Stock Exchange.

"Had I thought of it, I would have brought a stick from the Hundred Acre Wood and exchanged it for a city stick," said Pooh, looking up at the New York Stock Exchange sign.

"That's 'stock,' you silly bear," said Christopher Robin.

Pooh knew instantly that the stock market was an enchanted place. For its floors were not like the floors of the forest, gorse and bracken and heather, but carpeted with torn pieces of paper, and it echoed with the sound of scampering feet running this way and that. Standing there in the New York Stock Exchange, he saw the future of the world. He saw what lay in store for himself, his friends, and those who one day might be his friends.

And then Pooh smiled, for he knew then how he should invest his small fortune. He would not shutter a small company like Rabbit. And he certainly would not become a day trader like Tigger. No, Pooh knew exactly what to do.

From high above his perch in the visitor's gallery, he opened all seventeen pots of honey and spilled them over the rail, drippley-drappley, onto the computers and stock tickers below. The honey oozed over the circuit boards. It smothered the silicon chips. It slithered into the hard drives.

The computers fizzled and made a hummy little noise, then no longer were. The entire stock market had become mired in wonderful, golden, delicious honey, so much so that no business would be conducted for at least a month and a day, enough time for Pooh's friends to regain their senses. For Rabbit to become Rabbit. For Tigger to become . . . well, Tigger.

"Oh, bear," said Christopher Robin as they left the New York Stock Exchange hand in hand, past screaming technicians, weeping stockbrokers, and numbed captains of industry. "How I do love you!"

"So do I," said Pooh.

# PART THREE

# America the *Odd*

# America, the Beautiful . . . and Odd . . . and Hysterical . . . and . . .

Well, this is embarrassing. I'd gone into a bank and simply because I wore a ski mask, packed heat, and gave the teller a note demanding she hand me over all the money, everyone now thinks I'm a bank robber.

I can explain. I'm a money tester. I take money from various banks and spend it in shops and restaurants to see if their $5, $10, and $20 bills work. So far, they all have. No, it's not a job you'll see advertised on Careerbuilder.com. I created the industry.

The fact is, I never would have been nabbed had I not left behind a copy of my Nobel Prize–winning acceptance speech, the one I got for furthering the Jokes and Anecdotes Arts and Sciences. The one with the words: "This is the property of Andy Simmons (5'9", 155 pounds, brown hair, brown eyes, flecks of spinach in teeth), humor editor of *Reader's Digest*, 750 3rd Avenue, New York City, NY 10017, 4th floor."

The end result is that I have now joined the ranks of the dumb criminal, one of America's most beloved characters. As a humor editor, I've made a good living off these ne'er-do-wells. Whenever I needed to fill a page, I'd find a passel of them and, presto! Job completed.

When I wasn't trading in dumb criminals, I produced exposés on other dolts, such as those people who think a lame excuse won't be seen for what it really is: a lame excuse. Work gaffes are also always a favorite; after all, nothing makes us happier than the knowledge that someone is less competent than ourselves. Of course we don't just go after foolish mistakes. Oddball has a lot of currency in our pages. That's why I've made sure to put pieces in this chapter about weird scientists, offbeat town names, and most bizarre of all—the American male (that's right, I'm ratting out my own kind!).

Yes, America is the land of the odd peccadillo, and I like a good peccadillo, because it's something that this country is stocked up on. And in a time of depleted natural resources, I'm glad we have something of value to mine. Because if I'm anything, I'm a patriot! Dumb criminals, lame excuses— they're like jazz, a homegrown art form. Sure, other countries have proudly trotted out their dumbest and dimmest in order to lay claim to the crown, and many of them are represented here. A special hats-off in particular to the Brits, who always give it a jolly good show. Like the time Londoner Joanna Kirchmeier arrived home only to find her husband, Helmut, in front of a mirror "just staring at himself, his pupils tiny." Helmut, a newly trained hypnotist, had accidentally hypnotized himself while rehearsing a new act and had been standing like that for five hours.

Yes, good try, Britain, but I think even you will agree that when it comes to oddballs, it's U-S-A! U-S-A! U-S-A!!

# My American Journey (Part 1)

I was holed up in Boring, Oregon, thinking about trying someplace different. I had no good reason, so I traveled to Why, Arizona, to figure things out.

I kicked around a few days until I found the answer. It was in *Why Not*, Mississippi. I quickly drove off to *Jot 'Em Down*, Texas, to make sure I wouldn't forget it. I needed a town that had some life to it. So I jumped in the car, set the GPS, and didn't stop until I reached *Spunky Puddle*, Ohio.

It was spunky all right. I was so happy, I danced the night away to *Twistville*, West Virginia, and *Disco*, Tennessee. I boogied until my shoes wore down. Soon, I walked gingerly over to *Loafers Glory*, North Carolina, to buy a new pair. I was looking pretty sharp, sharp enough to stop in *Handsome Eddy*, New York. Eddy wasn't around, but I knew where to find him—in *Loveladies*, New Jersey, where all the women, it seemed, were looking for *Husband*, Pennsylvania.

It was a tough town. One gal told me my romancing needed some work, that I should practice in *Sweet Lips*, Tennessee. I was heartbroken. I skipped *Intercourse*, Pennsylvania, altogether and headed straight to *Lonelyville*, New York. I needed a stiff drink and knew where to get one—*Rum Center*, Louisiana. I wanted more, so I hit *The Bottle*, Alabama. After draining the last drop, I found myself in *Condemned Bar*, California. If I continued like this I was headed straight to . . . *Hell*, Michigan.

After a few hours in *Satan's Kingdom*, Vermont—and

an hour running for my life in *Goblintown*, Virginia—I felt a little more like myself. So I had a pick-me-up in *Egg Nog*, Utah, which got me back to *Merry Hell*, Mississippi. All right, maybe it was more than one drink, because I woke up in *Cranky Corner*, Louisiana. If only I'd taken that detour to *Cut Off*, Louisiana!

I was starving. I grabbed breakfast in *Oatmeal*, Texas, lunch in *Sandwich*, Massachusetts, and dessert in *Pie Town*, New Mexico. If I knew what was good for me I'd have stopped after *Greasy*, Oklahoma, because I was feeling pretty sick by the time I left *Lick Skillet*, Tennessee.

I was mad at myself for acting like an idiot. I knew I wouldn't be welcomed at my next destination, *Brilliant*, Ohio. No, that was for some *Edison*, New Jersey, type. When I got lost on my way to *Dumbell*, Wyoming, it dawned on me—I had to cease my wandering ways. I parked in *Do Stop*, Kentucky, took out the map, and found where I would soon call home. I didn't need *Wealthy*, Texas, nor *Fame*, West Virginia. I'd find everything I could possibly need in a place called . . . *Happyland*, Oklahoma.

# Lessons I Learned from Dumb Criminals— All Too True Edition

Do you enjoy being hounded by law enforcement and mingling with lowlifes? Does jail sound fun? If you answered, "Why, yes!" to both of those questions, then a life of crime might just be the right career for you! So, here are a few tips— along with some cautionary-but-true tales—to get you started!

## Pick the Right Equipment!

Bringing a weapon to a crime causes more grief than it's worth. But if you do decide to arm yourself, it ought to be with something that will actually scare someone. In 2008, this year, nineteen-year-old Justin MacGilfrey allegedly entered a Daytona Beach, Florida, store, pointed his index finger at the clerk, cocked his thumb, and demanded all the money in the register.

The clerk assumed it was a joke. But MacGilfrey, who has pleaded not guilty to robbery, was serious. After determining the finger wasn't loaded, the clerk emerged from behind the register. That's when the finger-slinger holstered his digit and ran from the store. He was later arrested and, presumably, fingerprinted. (The charges were eventually dropped.)

## The Police Don't Care for Criminal Types

So don't initiate a relationship like Phillip Williams did. He was an unhappy consumer, so he stopped two Tampa, Florida, police officers, handed over his crack pipe, and asked if they wouldn't mind testing the crack cocaine that he'd bought earlier, just to make sure it was the real deal. Good news! It was. Bad news! They arrested him.

A seventeen-year-old suspected arsonist approached a car in Lambertville, Michigan, intending to siphon gas from it. What he forgot to do was ask permission from the detective sitting in the front seat.

## Take the Time to Come Up with the Perfect Alias

The best criminals all have colorful aliases. Names like Jimmy Nostrils and Joe Bananas really liven up a criminal's résumé. Look what happens if you don't have one prepared.

When Sheboygan, Wisconsin, police pulled over a car for not having proper registration, a passenger did what many criminals do—he supplied the cops with an alias. Bad move. Turns out that particular alias was wanted for vehicular homicide.

Steve Lent was pulled over in Peekskill, New York, for a traffic violation. Since there was already an outstanding warrant for his arrest, he passed himself off as his brother, Christopher. What he'd forgotten was that there was an arrest warrant out for Christopher, too.

## Do Your Homework

Remember! Whether your crime calls for aliases or an elaborate fraud, do a little background research so you don't end up like Alexander D. Smith, who walked into an Augusta, Georgia, bank and tried to open an account with a one million dollar bill. Great—except there is no such thing as a one million dollar bill. (Smith was given a psychiatric evaluation.)

Some surveillance would have saved a lot of grief for the two machete-wielding men who barged into a Sydney, Australia, bar demanding money. They didn't know the club was hosting a bikers' meeting. One robber ended up in the hospital, and the other hog-tied with electrical wire.

## Make the Cops Work for a Living

In general, broadcasting one's whereabouts is a bad idea. Convicted of receiving stolen property, James Wombles, age thirty-seven, had to wear an ankle bracelet as part of his parole. The bracelet came complete with a GPS monitoring system that let cops track his every move. Over the course of a few weeks, the Riverside, Ohio, man allegedly broke into six homes. You know where this is going—just as the cops knew where Wombles was going. Following the signals from his bracelet, they tracked him to his car, where they found him sitting on the stolen booty.

## There Are These People Called Lawyers

They help people who have been arrested. If you are ever arrested, get a lawyer and let him or her do all the talking for you. Unlike Ellis Cleveland, who was arrested in Honolulu and informed by a detective that he was suspected of robbing four banks.

"Four?" responded an irate Cleveland, according to the detective's affidavit. "I didn't do four; I only robbed three banks."

## Lie Low

Publicity is great for starlets. But criminals really should shun the spotlight.

Robert Echeverria, age thirty-two, scammed a Rialto, California, Del Taco by calling up and pretending he was a local CEO whose order had been botched. Echeverria was so pleased with the $15 in free eats, he and two friends shot a short movie called "How to Scam Del Taco" and posted it on YouTube. It proved popular, especially among cops, who watched it and then arrested the would-be executive.

## Remember! Don't Focus Attention On Yourself

Consumers in northern Alabama became suspicious when they received recorded messages urging them to go to a website where they could update their bank account records. How did victims know it was just a "phishing" expedition? Their caller IDs read, "This is a scam."

> Their caller IDs read, "This is a scam."

## Have a Plan

No matter what venture you undertake, have an exit strategy. Receiving a report of a man banging on a door at three thirty in the morning, police responded to a mini-mart in Ossining, New York. When officers arrived, they chased Blake Leak, age twenty-three, through the streets and down an embankment. It looked bleak for Leak until both cops took a tumble. Seizing the opportunity, he sought refuge on the grounds of a large building.

Unfortunately, it turned out to be a well-known local landmark, the Sing Sing maximum-security prison, where he was nabbed by a guard.

## Remember! Once You Make a Plan, Don't Deviate From It

Scottish shoplifter Aron Morrison was picked up after pinching a bottle of vodka from a liquor store. It didn't take Sherlock Holmes to find Morrison, especially since he'd left his name and phone number with the clerk after asking her out on a date.

## Beware of Witnesses

Good criminals arrange it so no one is aware that a crime has taken place. Last year, a German psychologist allegedly took advantage of three of his patients. He had sex with one, named Kathrin; convinced another, Finja, to buy him some shoes and shirts; and conned the third, Leonie, into cleaning his house and paying for his vacations. This all came to light when a fourth patient, Monika, became suspicious and called the police. Why would she do that when the three victims hadn't? Because the four are one person: Kathrin, Finja, and Leonie are Monika's multiple personalities. When Monika confronted the psychologist, he refused to discuss the matter, saying it would violate therapist-client confidentiality, something he owed all his clients, including alter egos.

## Remember! Don't Leave Incriminating Evidence at the Crime Scene

A convenience-store robber in Des Moines, Iowa, got away with $115 but left his coat. Inside: his W-2 tax form.

A Target store clerk in Augusta, Georgia, agreed to take back a printer from a dissatisfied customer, then noticed some property the customer had left in the machine: counterfeit bills.

After getting into an argument with a woman at a bus stop, Justin John Boudin of St. Paul, Minnesota, punched her in the face. He then attacked a Good Samaritan with a folder, which fell to the ground when Boudin fled. But cops tracked him down, thanks to what was inside that folder: his anger-management homework.

# Liar, Liar

"Of course I complete the Saturday *New York Times* crossword puzzle . . . in pen!"

"I never check out my exes on Facebook."

"No, I don't mind sitting outside the ladies' changing room in Macy's while you try on the entire spring collection."

Admit it. You lie. And if you say you don't, you're a liar. We all lie, as often as two or three times every ten minutes, says one study (if it can be trusted). Sounds pretty reprehensible, right? But consider the alternative.

"You can't stop lies entirely," University of Massachusetts psychologist Robert Feldman told *US News & World Report*. "Society would grind to a halt." That's because most of us fib to spare feelings—ours and others'. Too much truth hurts. Case in point: When *Cosmopolitan* asked readers for dates-from-hell stories, a guy named Don revealed the pain he felt when his blind date announced, "Your brother is so hot . . . you guys look nothing alike."

But while most of us fib to avoid such hard-heartedness, others lie . . . like rugs. And not even good rugs, more like the cheap ones you get in the remainder bins at Pier One stores. Take the Brazilian soccer player who claimed he'd been kidnapped just so he could avoid a fine for being late to practice. He was arrested for falsely reporting a crime.

What was this dolt thinking?

He wasn't, says Cornell University professor Jeff Hancock. Consider this mathematical equation:

Desperation + lack of time = idiotic lie. People like him, says Hancock, "should never again put themselves in the position of having to lie on the spot," for the simple reason that they stink at it. Thank God, otherwise I might be out of a job.

The worst liars are a font of humor. I don't know about you, but I listen to their stream of ridiculousness and wonder how far they're willing to go. And you've got to hand it to them, they don't disappoint. Why leave well enough alone when you can build castles in the sky? Just like these fibbers . . .

## What the Fashionable Criminal Is Wearing

When Eugene Todie pulled up to the New York–Canada border, guards noticed that he was sporting the latest in criminal haute couture, an ankle monitor. Intrigued, they asked Todie, "What's the occasion?"

**The lie:** Todie explained that a friend urged him to wear it as a show of solidarity with Lindsay Lohan, who was following a court order and wearing one herself.

**Were there any suckers?** After a background check showed that Todie was on probation for criminal contempt and not allowed to leave the country, he was arrested.

## NSF(W)

A few years ago, several staffers at the National Science Foundation (NSF) in Washington, DC, were investigated for watching porn on their computers at work. The biggest perpetrator: an executive who'd spent 331 days chatting online with naked women, reported the *Washington Times*. But government money—up to $58,000—was not wasted, insisted the man.

**The lie:** By clicking on the various porn sites, our executive provided these women with a living. "He explained that these young women were from poor countries and needed to make money to help their parents, and this site helped them do it," an investigator reported.

**Were there any suckers?** His altruism notwithstanding, the official has since "retired." In light of his actions, the foundation has tightened controls to filter out inappropriate Internet addresses.

## Deceit 101

While running for a seat on the Birmingham, Alabama, Board of Education, twenty-three-year-old Dr. Antwon B. Womack said he'd graduated from West End High School and received a bachelor's degree in elementary education from Alabama A&M. Impressive, except that Womack was twenty-one, didn't have a doctorate, didn't attend college, and never graduated from high school. Other than that, he told the *Birmingham News*, he was honest.

**The lie:** "My campaign is not based on a foundation of lies," he insisted.

**The truth:** "It's just that the information I provided to the people is false."

**The honest-to-God truth:** The revelations are "really going to hurt my career."

**Were there any suckers?** Yes, 117 of them. That's how many people voted for Womack, landing him in fourth place out of five candidates.

## Pork, the Other Banned Substance

Clenbuterol is a drug used by farmers to keep their animals from getting too chubby. Because athletes don't want to waddle across the finish line, some are tempted to try it, even though the International Olympic Committee has banned its use. But when Tong Wen, China's Olympic judo champion, tested positive for clenbuterol in 2010 after an event, her coach had an explanation for how it ended up in Tong's system.

**The lie:** She ate "a lot of pork chops," the coach told the BBC. And that pork was tainted by clenbuterol.

**Were there any suckers?** Olympic officials are famously vigilant. In 1998, when track star Dennis Mitchell made the claim that lots of sex and beer were responsible for his high levels of testosterone, the International Association of Athletics Federations banned him from racing for two years. But Tong's blame-the-pig defense panned out, sort of. She was cleared by the Court of Arbitration for Sport because of a technicality: She wasn't present when a backup urine sample was tested. The International Judo Federation blasted the ruling, insisting it would have "a very negative influence" on the sports world.

## A Crash Course in Lying

When Jayson Williams's Mercedes-Benz SUV crashed in Manhattan, officers found the former basketball star sitting in the passenger seat. When asked by police who'd caused the crash, Williams deflected all blame.

**The lie:** It wasn't me, he insisted. "Someone else was driving."

**Were there any suckers?** The fact that witnesses had seen Williams behind the wheel, not to mention the absence of anyone else in the car, led authorities to conclude that he'd switched seats. And yes, alcohol was involved.

## Is It a Dat or a Cog?

Landlord Barry Maher has a strict rule against dogs in his Santa Barbara, California, building. Cats? Fine. Dogs? Nope. So when neighbors complained about a barking dog, Maher called the tenant.

**The lie:** "Oh, I would never have a dog," she told him.

**The bigger lie:** "What I have is a special breed of cat."

**The whopper:** "It's a dog-cat. A mix of a dog and a cat."

**Were there any suckers?** Almost. "It was so crazy that I actually wondered, *Is there really such a thing as a dog-cat?*" Maher told realestate.msn.com. There isn't. So tenant and dog-cat were evicted.

## Plane Stupid

Sergei Berejnoi raced through Denver International Airport trying to catch his SkyWest Airlines flight. Unfortunately, he arrived just after the plane had left the gate with his luggage onboard. With his pleas to bring back the plane falling on deaf ears, he offered the gate agent a not-so-subtle reason for doing as he said.

**The lie:** "There's a bomb in my suitcase."

**Were there any suckers?** The aircraft was checked for explosives. When none were found, Berejnoi took a trip of another sort, to the police station. He received six months probation.

## Just Desserts

Two years ago, an Iowa bar was cited for serving alcohol to a minor; specifically, a minor was served a vodka-infused Jell-O shot.

**The lie:** Jell-O shots are not alcoholic beverages, the bar owners insisted. Once they become gelatinous globs, the shots are a dessert.

**Were there any suckers?** In her ruling, the judge—an apparent Jello-O-phile—opined: "While there might be some debate as to whether Jell-O is a food item or a beverage, the Jell-O shots served by the licensee were alcoholic beverages." In other words, the dessert has one thing in common with booze—it'll get you blotto.

# Calling Dr. Frankenstein!

While innovation is what got us through the Dark Ages, polio, and Celine Dion, some scientists and inventors have stumbled in their efforts to move us forward.

Indeed, when I consider the great scientists, I think of such Nobel laureates as Curie, Einstein, Whitcome . . . What? You've never heard of Katherine K. Whitcome? You mean you missed the paper by the University of Cincinnati assistant professor and her colleagues explaining why pregnant women don't tip over? She, too, is a laureate—an Ig Nobel laureate. The tongue-in-cheek Ig Nobels are presented annually by the Harvard-based magazine *Annals of Improbable Research*. Far more entertaining than the Oscars and a more pleasurable experience than the Stinkiest Cheese in the World Contest, these honors are bestowed upon those men and women—American and otherwise—who dabble in some very strange science, and they're the best awards in the world. Here are some of my favorite past winners.

## Public Health Prize

Elena N. Bodnar, Raphael C. Lee, and Sandra Marijan of Chicago, Illinois, invented a brassiere that, in an emergency, can be converted into a pair of protective face masks—one for the wearer and one to be given to a lucky bystander.

It appears that in the face of chemical or biological warfare, a woman's primary job is to doff her clothes. The face-mask bra isn't some tactic of the porn industry. Instead, it's intended for anyone who may come in contact with dangerous fumes. Masks, say the inventors, may not be available, but there's almost always a bra handy. The cups are made of air filters and can be disconnected, then shared. The woman can easily strap it over her nose and mouth "to help purify the inhaled air," reads the report, "while keeping her hands free," presumably to fend off unwanted suitors.

## Peace Prize

Stephan Bolliger, Steffen Ross, Lars Oesterhelweg, Michael Thali, and Beat Kneubuehl of the University of Bern, Switzerland, for determining which hurts more: being smashed over the head with a full bottle of beer or with an empty bottle.

An inherent problem in an experiment of this nature is finding volunteers who will agree to be brained with a beer bottle in the name of science. The scientists overcame this obstacle by dropping steel balls onto full and empty beer bottles. They found that the empties were sturdier than their full brethren because the gas pressure from the liquid produces additional strain on the glass.

Needless to say, full or not, beer bottles can cause a whole lot of hurt, which is why the scientists advocate prohibiting them "in situations [that] involve risk of human conflicts." Of course, if we outlaw beer bottles, only outlaws will drink beer from bottles.

## Medicine Prize

Donald L. Unger of Thousand Oaks, California, won for investigating a possible cause of arthritis of the fingers, by cracking the knuckles of his left hand—but never the knuckles of his right hand—twice a day for sixty years.

After being warned by his mother to swear off that demon knuckle cracking, young Donald Unger tested the accuracy of this hypothesis on himself. More than 219,000 cracked knuckles later, the verdict is in: Crack away. Unger could detect no difference between the two hands, and he found no evidence of arthritis. From why you shouldn't run with scissors to why you should wait an hour after eating before you swim, Unger's seminal research has thrown everything our mothers told us into question.

## Veterinary Medicine Prize

Catherine Douglas and Peter Rowlinson of Newcastle University, United Kingdom, proved that cows that have names give more milk than cows that are nameless.

Admit it, when was the last time you paid a compliment to a heifer? Or told one, "You're a thousand roast beef sand-wiches wrapped in a gorgeous leather jacket"? It turns out our attitudes make a difference. Being friendly and remem-bering a cow's name can increase milk yield by 258 liters a year. This came as no surprise to farmers, one of whom told the researchers that cows "hurt and love like anyone else."

## Chemistry Prize

Javier Morales, Miguel Apátiga, and Victor M. Castaño of Universidad Nacional Autónoma de México, for creating diamonds from tequila.

As if there weren't already enough reasons to love tequila! It seems we can spill a little on the bar and make diamonds. Of course, you have to heat it up to 536 degrees Fahrenheit and do a bunch of other stuff to it before you can place it on your main squeeze's finger. But the first round is on us!

## Biology Prize

Fumiaki Taguchi, Song Guofu, and Zhang Guanglei of Kitasato University Graduate School of Medical Sciences in Japan, for demonstrating that kitchen refuse can be reduced by more than ninety percent by using an enzyme-producing bacteria extracted from the feces of giant pandas.

While this has potential applications—reducing garbage and waste—it still raises the question, "How did it dawn on someone to try this experiment?" And, of course, if one of your aims in ridding yourself of garbage is to get rid of the stench, adding poop to it is not likely to help.

# Don't Call Us, We'll Call You

## Looking for a job? Be sure to proofread your résumé and cover letters.

Take the stress out of your job search by reading the gaffes of the dolts you're competing with. I strung some doozies together from resumania.com to create a résumé and cover letter that our HR department will no doubt hang on their secret wall of shame. Here's the result:

> *ANDY SIMMONS*
> *750 3RD AVE.*
> *NEW YORK, NY 10017*

*Dear Sir or Madman:*

*"I am sure you have looked through several résumés with the same information about work experience, education, and references. I am not going to give you any of that stuff."*

*"I would love to interview for the position of [insert job title here]. If you grant me an interview for [insert job title here], I feel confident you'll see why I'm the right person for the job." "My mother delivered me without anesthesia, so I have an IQ of 146 and can therefore learn anything."*

*"I enjoy working closely with customers, and my pleasant demeanor helps them feel comfortable and relaxed—not afraid." "I realize that my total lack of appropriate experience may concern those considering me for employment." But "I have integrity, so I will not steal office supplies and take them home."*

*"Please don't regard my fourteen positions as 'job-hopping.' I never once quit a job." "They stopped paying*

*me." "In my next life, I will be a professional backup dancer or a rabbi," but for now, "I am attacking my résumé for you to review." "I realize that my résumé is no longer exemplary thanks to my family destroying the computer file." Nevertheless, "here are my qualifications for you to overlook."*

*"Thank you for your consideration. Hope to hear from you shortly!"*

*Sincerely,*
*Andy Simmons*

---

### ANDY SIMMONS
### 750 3rd Ave., New York, NY 10017
### dolt@readersdigest.nitwit

**OBJECTIVE**
"Assertive, self-motivated, and goal-oriented individual seeks a position that utilizes my computer training and experience and/or bartending skills."

**EMPLOYMENT HISTORY**
**Last job:** "Restaurant manager. Cleaned and supervised employees."

**Job before that:** "CFO for a wholesaler of women's slacks. We also sold men's bottoms."

**And job before that:** "I worked in the store's men's department, stalking shirts and pants."

**And before that:** "Bum. Abandoned belongings and led nomadic lifestyle."

**First job:** "Administrative professional. I coordinated meetings, made travel arrangements, and assisted security staff with badgering."

## REFERENCES
* "Scott."
* "My girlfriend."
* "None. I've left a path of destruction behind me."

## SKILLS
* "Speak English and Spinach."
* "Excellent memory; strong math aptitude; excellent memory."
* "I can type without looking at thekeyboard."
* "The ability to use short bursts of muscle force to propel myself—as in jumping or sprinting or throwing an object."
* "Able to whistle while pretending to drink water at the same time."

## INTERESTS
* "Gossiping."
* "Michael Bolton."

## EDUCATION
"Moron University"
"Attended collage courses."
Academic Achievement: "Received the Smith Schlorship Award."

---

# So Sue Me!

**WARNING!!! Reading this book may cause paper cuts. Opening this book and pressing it hard against the mouth and nose can cause suffocation. Because of this book's diminutive size, you might be tempted to swallow it. Do not! You could choke on the covers!**

Sorry about the above statement, but our legal department insisted on it. You can't be too safe. After all, while Americans hate lawyers, we love lawsuits—especially the crazy ones.

Take the case of the Lodi, California, city employee who accidentally drove a dump truck into Curtis Gokey's parked truck. Gokey sued the city, even though he was the Lodi, California, city employee driving the dump truck.

For some injured parties, no law need even be broken before they wield the lawyer card. In Jurupa, California, a retired Navy Reserve captain threatened to sue her colleagues on the school board if they didn't address her by her military title. And a while back, a father took his son's Little League coach to court over a losing season.

Any chance we'll all wake up one morning and decide to settle our differences over a nice cup of tea instead of going all lawsuity? Doubtful. Litigation is big business, costing American citizens and corporations $247 billion in 2006, or 1.87 percent of the gross domestic product. Don't believe us? Talk to our lawyer.

## Protect Me From Myself

The two prisoners waited to make their move until the guards left wing 4B, the maximum-security section of

Colorado's Pueblo County Jail. Then they slid open their defective cell doors, collected bedsheets and mattress covers from other inmates, and headed to the showers. There they pried off a broken ceiling tile and climbed into a vent, which led them to the roof via a door that was latched from the inside. Once on the roof, the prisoners, Scott Anthony Gomez Jr. and Oscar Mercado, tied the sheets and mattress covers together into a makeshift rope, secured it to a gas pipe, and began to rappel down the northwest side of the jail.

That's when the Great Escape of '07 went to hell in a handbasket. Gomez slipped and fell forty feet, injuring himself. He was rushed to the hospital, and Mercado was caught soon after.

So how did Gomez while away the hours during his recovery? By filing a lawsuit against the county board of commissioners, sheriff, and guards—for as much as the law would allow—on the grounds that they made it too easy for him to escape. He should know, since this was his second attempt. In his suit, Gomez claimed that the cell doors opened too easily and that guards vacated their posts and ignored information that a jailbreak was nigh. They were practically begging him to break out, he insisted. And who was he to disappoint?

"The defendants knew or should have known that the jail was not secure," read his complaint. "Furthermore, defendants knew that the plaintiff had a propensity to escape."

**Disposition:** Gomez couldn't escape the fact that he didn't have a case, which the judge tossed out in 2008.

## Justice Desserts

Prison, it turns out, is a great place to learn about tort law. Three inmates from the Kane County Jail in Illinois sued the county sheriff and Aramark food services in 2007 for supplying prisoners with subpar food, including soggy cookies and cakes.

> **Prison, it turns out, is a great place to learn about tort law.**

The two million dollars they sought would buy them a nice drying rack for their desserts.

**Disposition:** No Mrs. Fields for these prisoners—the judge dismissed the case.

## Quick, Switch to ER!

It's a fact: The squeamish should not watch NBC's reality show *Fear Factor*. With contestants eating worms and sitting in rat-filled tanks, it's best for the faint of heart to stick with the Watching Paint Dry channel.

Austin Aitken is one such couch potato. According to the Cleveland, Ohio, paralegal, a 2005 episode was so disgusting it literally made him ill. His blood pressure rose, and he grew dizzy, causing him to bang his head against a doorway as he fled the room. A $2.5 million payout from the television network, Aitken figured, would put him on the road to recovery.

**Disposition:** A judge assumed that it was for occasions such as these that the remote was invented and threw the case out of court.

## My Problem Is, I Love Too Much

A county Republican chairman in Florida said his bid to head the state party was sabotaged by a letter falsely accusing him of having been married six times. Jim Stelling claims that the letter, sent to state party leaders implied that he had loose moral standards and therefore was not suitable for the position. So he sued the letter's author, Nancy Goettman, for defamation. Why? Because he hadn't been married six times—only five.

"I believe in family values," Stelling insisted to the judge. **Disposition:** In 2005, a judge ruled in Stelling's favor. But probably figuring that once you've been married five times, it might as well be six, he nixed awarding Stelling any money.

## A Legal Wedgie

The customer's pants must have really been something. After all, he leveled a $67 million lawsuit against a dry cleaner for losing them. Maybe Roy L. Pearson just wanted to flex his legal muscle. You see, he's not your average pants wearer—he's also an administrative law judge for the District of Columbia.

It all started two years ago, when Judge Pearson took a pair of pants to Custom Cleaners to have them altered for the sum of $10.50. Two days later, the pants turned up missing. Pearson told the Chungs, the family who owns the cleaners, to cough up a thousand bucks for a new suit. A week later, the Chungs said the pants had showed up, and they refused to pay. But Pearson said the pants weren't his and decided to sue. The Chungs countered with a $12,000 settlement offer—that would have amounted to twelve brand-new sets of pinstripes for the judge. But out of principle, Pearson went ahead with his suit. Signs hanging in the store read Satisfaction Guaranteed and Same-Day Service, which he insisted constituted fraud.

How did he arrive at his princely sum? By following DC's consumer-protection laws, which impose fines of

$1,500 per violation, per day. Pearson figured he'd been cheated twenty different ways, twelve of them over the course of twelve hundred days, the length of time he estimated the offending signs were up. He then multiplied that amount by three, the number of Chungs who own the shop. His laundry list of greed included $1,500,000 for emotional damages and $542,500 to cover the cost of his lawyer, who happened to be a guy named Judge Roy L. Pearson. For good measure, he tacked on $45,000, the cost of renting a car for the next ten years to drive to and from some other dry cleaner.

**Disposition:** Even Pearson must have thought $67 million was a lot to ask for, since he dropped some of his demands before going to trial and ended up asking for only $54 million. That paltry sum was still too much for the presiding judge, who dismissed the case.

## Blonde Ambition

Charlotte Feeney says blondes have more fun, and that's why she sued cosmetics giant L'Oréal for $15,000. Feeney insisted her life was ruined when she accidentally touched up her naturally flaxen locks with brown dye from a mislabeled box.

"I was sick to my stomach," she said in an affidavit. "I have a bad hair day every day. I had headaches. I don't like myself. I stay home more than ever in my life. I wear hats most of the time." What's more, she told her doctor that she doesn't know how to dress now that she's no longer a blonde—one reason her doctor prescribed medication to treat anxiety and depression.

So why didn't she dye her hair blond and wait for her natural color to grow back? Who knows, but the real question is, "What's wrong with being a raven-haired beauty?"

"Blondes get more attention than brunettes," she claimed. "Emotionally, I miss that."

**Disposition:** No doubt an Audrey Hepburn fan, the judge dismissed the suit, ruling that Feeney never proved that L'Oréal was to blame for the mix-up.

## ePay Up

Ask Steve Shellhorn and he'll probably tell you that if you have nothing nice to say about someone, lie. Shellhorn, a Seattle native, bought coins on eBay from Charles Burgess, who then asked for feedback (a regular practice on the site). Was the service good or bad? Shellhorn was torn. The Morgan silver dollars were in fine shape, and the price was fair. But the packaging left a lot to be desired.

> Charlotte Feeney says blondes have more fun, and that's why she sued cosmetics giant L'Oréal for $15,000.

"The coins were hanging out of the envelope," he later told Seattle's *King 5 News*. There should have been proper packing to keep them in place. With that in mind, Shellhorn left neutral feedback, neither good nor bad.

The lukewarm response got a hot one from Burgess. Charging fraud and extortion, he sued Shellhorn for $10,000 over his "childish and vindictive" behavior, which, he feared, could harm future sales.

**Disposition:** Misery loves company, and Shellhorn had plenty. It turns out that Burgess made it a habit to go after less-than-thrilled customers. The judge sided with Shellhorn, but not before he'd spent $500 for an attorney.

## Air Apparent

A lot of men wouldn't mind being mistaken for Michael Jordan. After all, Jordan is famous and handsome, not to mention the greatest basketball player of all time. Allen Heckard, however, begs to differ. After being told he resembled His Airness one too many times, he sued Jordan and the chairman of Nike, Phil Knight, for $832 million. Imagine what he would have demanded had people thought he had a face like Larry Bird's.

Like Jordan, Heckard is African American and bald, and wears a hoop in one ear and Air Jordans on his feet. He also likes to play basketball. For you nitpickers, Heckard is six inches shorter than Jordan, eight years older, and much lighter in the wallet. But that's neither here nor there. For fifteen years, he'd been identified as Michael Jordan, and someone had to pay for defamation, permanent injury, and his emotional pain and suffering.

Now, it's obvious what Jordan's role was in making this man's life miserable, but what was Phil Knight's crime? Well, he promoted Jordan and made him—and, ipso facto, Heckard—one of the most recognizable people in the world.

Still, what's so awful about looking like Mike? According to foxsports.com, Heckard claims that it's saddled him with a level of professional expectations that he's unable to live up to. Heckard, by the way, is an airport shuttle-bus driver.

**Disposition:** Maybe resembling Michael Jordan isn't so bad after all, since Heckard dropped the lawsuit without giving a reason.

# The Guide to the American Man-Hug

The man-hug is a vestigial practice of a bygone era when men sought to show off their feminine side by toting purses, wearing paisley, and pretending to like Joni Mitchell.

I, like most American males, am personally opposed to greeting other males with a cuddle. We guys would prefer a nod, a punch in the arm, or, better yet, to let our wives do the hugging for us. Our European brothers are different. Given the opportunity, they will hug anything—women, men, children, fire hydrants. . . . If they can wrap their arms around it, it's in danger of being embraced. Still, even in the good ol' USA, I'll occasionally run into someone who's just come back from Italy or an Olive Garden and feels compelled to greet me with arms akimbo. Should that happen to you, here are some points to consider. But first, remember this: The act you are about to engage in is about as intimate as one American male gets with another American male (unless said male is a dog), and is therefore executed with the least amount of intimacy possible. Good luck.

## To Hug or Not?

You have milliseconds to answer these questions before deciding on a hug, a handshake, a wave, or fleeing: "Will the person I'm considering hugging be receptive?" "Will he sweat on me?" "Is that *him* swimming in Axe cologne?"

## "I'm Going or It!"

You've determined that it's his wife who's lathered on the Axe. Get ready to commence man-hug! Stand a good foot away. This no-man's land is the DMZ, a necessary barrier to ensure minimum intimacy. North Koreans know enough not to cross such a threshold, and so should you.

## The Hand Grab

Clasp the other man's hand as if you're about to arm wrestle. Instead of slamming it against a table, use it to draw him toward you.

## Uh-Oh, His Lips Are Getting Close . . .

Quickly turn your face forty-five degrees to the left. **Repeat:** *Turn your face forty-five degrees to the left!*

## The Back Pat

The pat is an important element because it lessens the amount of time you actually have to touch the other guy. **Remember:** You're not frisking him. It's a hearty pat, as if you're burping a baby: "There you go, let's get that beer out of ya. That's a good middle-aged man. . . ."

## How Long Must I Do This For?

Any longer than three beats and people will suggest you two rent yourselves a motel room.

## Okay, I Want Out

Push back, release your grip, smile embarrassedly, and pretend it never happened.

# Lame Excuses

**Well, that's just great. Not only does some governor in South Carolina have a tryst in Argentina, his staff uses my excuse.**

Now I can never again trot out the old hiking-the-Appalachian-Trail-so-I-couldn't-be-reached defense. I don't even like to hike, but I do like a good Argentinean tryst, and I really love a good excuse. We all do—that's why we reach for one whenever we're trapped. "Any excuse is better than none," says John Rooney, a professor emeritus in psychology at La Salle University, "because if you tell a good story and entertain, that's sometimes more important than the truth."

I'm all for that, as is the woman in Ohio who was arrested for torching a bar's bathroom. When asked by a cop why she did it, she stated unequivocally, "I felt stressed because of the death of Michael Jackson." That's certainly more entertaining than "I was blotto." And what about the Polish woman who insisted that her teenage daughter came down with a bad case of pregnancy after swimming in a hotel pool? Were you entertained, or did you think that it sounded plausible? If the latter, then you'll believe these excuses, which are among the best I've ever heard.

### "Frankly, I'm a Shallots Man Myself"

Peter Ivan Dunne was awaiting trial in Ireland, charged with a sex crime. Before the trial ended, he fled to England and was convicted in absentia. About to be extradited, he explained to a British court that he should not be sent back, because his experience with the Irish penal system had led him to believe that his right to life, as spelled out by Article 2 of the European Convention on Human Rights, would be violated.

**The lame excuse:** They'd serve him red onions. Dunne's allergic to them, and he was sure the prison would make him eat the "potentially life-threatening" vegetable.

**Did anyone buy it?** The court decided that it was doubtful that the prison would have such a cavalier attitude toward his allergy and shipped Dunne back to Ireland.

### "My Hands Are Clean—My Liver, Not So Much"

When in doubt, blame booze! Unless, of course, the drunk excuse only makes matters worse. A few years ago, then–New York congressman Vito Fossella was pulled over in Alexandria, Virginia, by a cop and blew a 0.17 on the Breathalyzer—more than twice the legal limit. After the hangover, Fossella knew he'd better start thinking fast.

**The lame excuse:** His high blood-alcohol level was a result of the alcohol-based hand sanitizer he'd used.

**Did anyone buy it?** After several "What do you take us for?" looks from the cops, DAs, the press—pretty much everyone—Fossella changed his plea from DUIHS (driving under the influence of hand sanitizer) to good old-fashioned DUI.

### "No Thong? No Candy? No Mr. Nice Guy!"

Marco Fella of England admitted attacking his girlfriend with a dog toy and, another time, biting her finger. But it wasn't his fault.

**The lame excuse:** "My client's temper snapped because he felt his partner was not making enough effort in the relationship," said his lawyer.

**The lamer excuse:** She wore baggy pants instead of the sexy thong he preferred.

**The lamerer excuse:** Biting and assault with a pet toy aside, Fella is not really violent—he just hadn't had his fill of Mars bars. See, Fella is a sugar addict and has a ten-Mars-bars-a-day habit. And if he's jonesing for one, well, he's not responsible for his actions.

**Did anyone buy it?** Possibly the Mars Inc., marketing division, but that's about it. Fella enrolled in an anger management course.

### "I Was Too Taxed to File"

Charles J. O'Byrne, the top aide to then New York governor David Paterson, neglected to file tax returns for five years. "Neglected" is really the wrong word, says his lawyer: O'Byrne *couldn't* pay his taxes.

> An APA representative told the *New York Times* that it doesn't recognize late-filing syndrome as a psychiatric condition.

**The lame excuse:** He suffers from a medical condition called late-filing syndrome, which is caused by depression. And even though this depression did not stop him from being a highly functional professional or enjoying an active social life, it did seem to affect his ability to pay taxes—five years in a row.

**Did anyone buy it?** Not the American Psychiatric Association. An APA representative told the *New York Times* that it doesn't recognize late-filing syndrome as a psychiatric condition.

### "Decimal Points Are So Confusing"

A $1,772.50 bank deposit showed up in Randy and Melissa Pratt's bank account as $177,250. No problem, said the Bloomsburg, Pennsylvania, couple. We'll just quit our jobs,

close up the house, and move to sunny Florida. Bye! Of course, banks hate to lose that much money, so they sicced the cops on the Pratts. But the couple swore they weren't thieves and that it had all been just an honest mistake.
**The lame excuse:** Her husband was a roofing installer, said Melissa Pratt, so they often got large checks. And, well, all large checks look alike, so they didn't pay such close attention, because, after all, who pays attention to a check for $177,250?
**Did anyone buy it?** Would you? Melissa Pratt pleaded guilty to theft, and Randy Pratt was awaiting trial at press time.

## The Lame Excuse Starter Script

Are you routinely in need of a good excuse, only to find yourself resorting to the same, tired retreads? If so, I've put together this handy script, using only tried-and-true whoppers that have served me well on countless occasions. In this scenario, I've created a confrontation between an employee and his employer. (Okay, okay, it's a transcript between me and my boss.) But these lame excuses work anywhere, so clip and save for easy reference.

**Employee:** Yes, sir, it's true that the words *big, fat idiot* were preceded by the words *you are a*. However, I assure you my words were "taken out of context."[1] But "I apologize if my comments offended."[2] "The truth is, I'm not perfect. This is not about perfection."[3] I understand that our harsh words stem from the fact that I neglected to get you the Frobisheyer contract this morning. But "I had other priorities."[4] Last night, I was busy with a friend. No, we don't have to tell my wife—"I was just giving her a ride home,"[5] that's all. But after what happened, HR insisted that I take a certain test, and, well, I didn't pass, you know, because of my "vanishing twin."[6] I believe I told you all about that. No? My bad. But I swear "I didn't inhale and never tried it again."[7] And no, there is nothing suspicious about those pills security found. I need them. "I have really bad menstrual cramps."[8] Yes, I'm aware that I am a man: I suffer sympathy cramps. Besides, I also need them because "I have severe acid reflux."[9] The police weren't convinced either. Then again, "the police, since my trouble, have not worked out for me."[10] But not to worry, I'll get that contract to you just as soon as my trial ends. No, I'm not sure when that will be, since "I didn't show up for court, because I didn't have a professional bodyguard."[11]

1. **Russell Crowe's representative**, after Crowe implied that Sharon Stone had had a face-lift and looked like a chimpanzee
2. **Kentucky senator Jim Bunning's** non-apology apology after saying that Supreme Court justice Ruth Bader Ginsburg would not survive her cancer
3. **Laurie David**, green queen and producer of *An Inconvenient Truth*, after it was revealed that she'd flown several times on a carbon-spewing private jet
4. **Dick Cheney** on why he avoided serving in Vietnam
5. **Eddie Murphy**, after he was pulled over by cops for picking up a transvestite prostitute
6. **Olympic cyclist Tyler Hamilton** explaining away blood-doping charges. He claims his twin sibling died in utero, so he has two kinds of blood in his body.
7. **Bill Clinton** on his attempt at smoking pot
8. **Nicole Richie** explaining why Vicodin was in her system after she was found driving the wrong way on a freeway

9. **Ashlee Simpson**, after she was caught lip-synching on *Saturday Night Live*

10. **O. J. Simpson** on why he didn't call the police to help him retrieve his stolen goods from a Las Vegas hotel room

11. **Courtney Love** on why she failed to appear for her hearing on a drug-possession charge

# My American Journey (Part 2)

**People often ask me how I became the humor editor at *Reader's Digest*. It's quite simple, really . . .**

It all started in *Mars*, California. The way everyone stared at me made me feel as if I were from a different planet. After a good look at my reflection in *Monkey's Eyebrow*, Kentucky, I saw why. I put on hold my vacation to *Prettyboy*, Maryland—a trim was in order. But where? *Tater Peeler*, Tennessee, it seemed, was the logical spot. I was wrong. The barbers in *Scissors*, Texas, made a valiant effort to save my do, but it was too late: I was left down in the dumps in *Bald Head*, Maine.

Comfort food was called for, and I found some in *Cookietown*, Oklahoma. After a month of indulgence, people wondered aloud if I were from *Chunky*, Mississippi. "I haven't seen such cellulite since *Sandy Mush*, North Carolina!" they howled. The fat jokes got to me, so I moved to where they would never dare call me that—*Big Bone*, Kentucky. It was pure fantasyland. During the day, I swam in *Ham Lake*, Minnesota; at night I dreamed I was in *King Arthur Court*, Tennessee. All was fine as long as I got home by midnight in *Cinderella*, West Virginia, and didn't tell anyone about seeing *Unicorn*, Pennsylvania. Had I let that slip out, they'd surely have sent me straight to *Looneyville*, Texas.

But having grown up in *Tightwad*, Missouri, I wasn't about to pay the outrageous one-way fare. No, I needed someplace cheap. Too scared to fly into *Eek*, Alaska, I found an alternative lifestyle in *Gay Meadows*, Alabama. I told stories about my haircut and stumbled upon a receptive audience in *Chuckle*, North Carolina, where they swore I would kill in *Humorist*, Washington. Who was I to argue? I wasn't from *Squabbletown*, California. I knew the *Reader's Digest* editor was also staying in Texas, so I rang her doorbell in *Ding Dong*.

And that, Dear Reader, is how I landed in South Dakota and in this *Jolly Dump*.

# PART FOUR

# I Work with Other Funny People*

*Though Not as Funny as Me

# Let Me Get My Red Pencil

**Every once in awhile, I get to try my hand at editing an article that's more than fifty words.**

The big editors don't always trust me with anything too long because I get bored easily and start coloring in the o's. But give me a case of Red Bull, a red pencil, a dictionary for beginners, and I'm raring to go.

Writers aren't perfect, even the big ones represented here, like P. J. O'Rourke or Jerry Lewis, and that's where I, as their editor, come marching in. For example, sometimes they're off with their punctuation. But then, so am I. Why, just the other day I toodled over to our copy editor Paul and complained, "There's a piece of lint in the middle of this sentence and I can't get rid of it." Banging his head against his desk, he moaned, "That's" *BANG* "not" *BANG* "lint" *BANG*, "that's" *BANG* "a" *BANG* "comma" *BANG*, "you" *BANG* "blithering" *BANG* ". . ." I never did find out what I was because by then he'd knocked himself out.

Something you have to understand about copy editors: They live to place commas. Oh, how they love it. Paul rings a little bell every time he successfully squeezes a comma into a sentence. I swear, sometimes working here is like working in a car dealership.

I know how they feel, though. I love hyphens—they

make punch lines stick out. And colons: They make punch lines stick out, too. Sometimes I'll add an exclamation mark, because exclamation marks mean something's funny! Really funny!! No, really, *really* (I also *love* italics) funny!!! But here's where I get messed up: (Ooh, a colon!). Is it an exclamation mark or an exclamation point? I'd ask Paul, but he's busy placing commas.

Now here's something most people don't know—editors have their own language. For example, STET is editor-talk for "keep this text" and is to be used after you've spilled half the ink in your ballpoint pen crossing something out and writing STUPID!! STUPID!!! STUPID!!!! (in this case, the exclamation points—or is it marks?—do not mean something is funny) next to it, only to realize a minute later that you've been reading the article upside down, and that if you just turned the page right side up, it's not so bad. STET!

I also like how STET sounds like STAT, which is very doctorish and adds to my daydreams during those long, tedious articles that are longer than fifty words.

Here are some more words in editor-speak: HED is the title. DEK is the subtitle. LED are the first few sentences. Clearly, these were conceived at a time before copy editors existed. Here is some new slang I'd like to add to the editorial lexicon:

**UGH:** This guy's life is weirder than mine.
**HIC:** I'm hitting the bottle if he doesn't get to the point soon.
**ZZZ:** I fell asleep halfway through the LED.
**KIL:** She's funnier than me. Delete before boss reads.
**SOS:** I just gave myself a paper cut.
**HEN:** Remember to buy eggs.

Here now are some of the funniest articles I've edited from people not named Andy Simmons. They chose names like Lenore Skenazy, Lance Contrucci, and Jimmy Tingle.

There's one other name in the mix, one that might sound a bit familiar. That's because he insists on using my last name. The guy goes by the name Matty Simmons and claims he's my father. The fact that I've seen him hanging around my mother since the day I was born and he paid for my college tuition lends some credence to his argument. Among his many accomplishments (like eating twenty-five cherrystone clams in under a minute), Dad is a movie producer. His films include *Animal House* and *Vacation*. And in this chapter, I'm reprinting an article he wrote for *Reader's Digest* regarding that great mystery: What, exactly, does a movie producer do?

People wonder if being his son is how I got into the ha-ha business, and I always respond, "Damn right!" Dad put me to work at *National Lampoon*, which he created so I would have something to do after school.

A lot of people shy away from nepotism; not me. I'm a big proponent of it. In fact, it's worked out so well for me, I wonder why everyone doesn't try it. I'm always shocked when someone admits that they got their job through hard work and perseverance. Why? I try to tell them that their life would have been far simpler had they only had a well-connected father. But they usually mumble something under their breath that includes the words *spoiled*, *brat*, and *firing squad*.

I've tried to repay the favor by using Dad in the pages of *Reader's Digest*. He's a font of stories. Like the odd memo he forwarded to me that his friend, writer/director Harold Ramis, received from a movie executive regarding a script Harold had worked on. The exec's request: "Can you tone down the subtlety?"

Dad also likes to collect weird stage directions from movie and TV scripts he's read. Here are some that we ran a few years ago:

- "The detective enters a room and finds a body. (You don't have to use a real dead body. You could use a dummy or give a real actor knock-out drops to make sure he was still and looked dead)."
- "Seeing the suspect drive off, the detective starts the motor of his car. First, he opens the door and gets in the car."
- "A very weird looking woman greets him at the door. She should be very gaunt and nervous, sort of like the MGM executive on this picture."
- "He is shot in the chest. It hurts."

But the best thing about Dad is that he knows where all the commas and punctuation are supposed to go. I pass his articles on to Paul, sit back, and watch him struggle to fit in a comma.

# The Petrified Woman!

BY LENORE SKENAZY

Stop! Are you about to eat a scoop of onion dip? It could cause meningitis. Showing some kids around work? For God's sake, keep them away from the stapler. Planning a walk? Bring plenty of water or you could end up in a coma!

And let's not even talk about what could happen if you take the kids to the mall and find yourselves contemplating an escalator ride. Suffice it to say, you should tie their shoes, insist they hold the handrail, place them in the center of the step, and say your prayers (but not on your knees, for obvious reasons).

"Perhaps most important, learn where the emergency shutoff button is so you can turn off the escalator if some-one gets trapped while riding," says an American Academy of Pediatrics report, ominously titled "Hidden Dangers and Child Safety."

That's right: If you want to be safe—and who doesn't?— every time you ride the escalator with a child, you should first make sure you can leap into action and slam off the calamitous contraption, mid-mangle.

That's not too much to think about when you're on a little shopping trip, is it?

I say it is. I say we are being warned about the weirdest, wildest, least likely, and most far-fetched, ill-founded, and downright bizarre possibilities to the point where we are being scared stupid. "Watch out" mania rules the media. As Ellen DeGeneres joked in her best newscaster voice, "It could be the most deadly thing in the world, and you may be having it for dinner. We'll tell you what it is tonight at eleven." With warnings coming at us thick and fast from every media source, and especially from Dr. Oz—a one-man worry machine—we are in danger (Danger!) of becoming too scared to even get off the couch and go to the bathroom . . . which is probably just as well because did you know there are germs lurking in the toilet bowl? Pretty scary!

All the warnings above are real; the stapler one came from a friend's interoffice memo. But they're just the tip of the iceberg. (Watch out for those, too!) For about a month, I watched TV, cruised the Internet, and read a bunch of books, magazines, and e-mail "tips" to see what the average American gets warned about in the course of everyday life.

The result? I am typing this from inside a giant safe-deposit box. You can feed me—but no onion dip, please—from a hole I drilled in the side.

I don't have a cell phone, because it could give me a brain tumor. I don't have a bottle of water, because the plastic could disrupt my endocrine receptors and turn me into a woman. Oh, wait. I already am.

Well . . . see?

I don't have a mattress, because the fumes could be toxic. I don't eat meat; it could give me asthma. I can't have a pet; I could trip over it. I can't wash my hair, because shampoo could be carcinogenic (and also because I'm in a box). But I can't leave the box and go to the grocery store, because I might be tempted to put my kid in a shopping cart. And according to the American Academy of Pediatrics, "parents are strongly encouraged to seek alternatives to transporting their child in a shopping cart until an effective revised performance standard for shopping cart safety is implemented in the United States."

That's right: The modern American shopping cart is just

too dangerous. Parents must come up with an alternative.
Maybe a dogsled? A mini Hummer? A kid-size version of
those exercise balls you put ger-
bils in to roll around?

Oh, well, I probably shouldn't
leave my box anyway, because
if I go out in the sun, it could
give me cancer. Then again, so
could sunscreen. Then again . . .
Oh, heck, I'm not really in a box.

> "I probably shouldn't leave my box anyway, because if I go out in the sun, it could give me cancer."

That was just a bit of hyperbole, a trick I learned from the
warning industry itself. It works this way: The media will
dig up some new study or, alternatively, find some tragic
example of something really strange that may sort of prove
that someone somewhere is somehow in at least a smidgen
of danger. The next thing you know, it's "Why you should
never _____ [fill in a verb]." Or "Up next! Is
your _____ [fill in a noun] dangerous?" The
answer to the latter is always yes!

Let's take a look at some of the warnings out there:

## Watch Out for Dip!

Dr. Oz was celebrating Super Bowl Sunday, or, as he said
his family likes to call it, "Super Germ Sunday."

What fun they must be.

Anyway, Dr. Oz had some woman serve dip at her
church, and then he sent the dip remains to a lab to see
what was in it, besides the inevitable onion soup mix.

Guess what. The lab discovered Group B streptococcus,
bacteria generally found in the intestinal tract that can
probably be traced to the detested double-dippers.
Furthermore, said Dr. Oz, these bacteria can lead to
things like . . . meningitis!

He neglected to add that strep B is usually a hazard only to newborns (who aren't big dip enthusiasts), and bacterial meningitis is quite rare. Instead, he left viewers ready to lynch the next guy who sticks a half-chomped chip in the guacamole.

But it's not just dip that's going to kill you. Dr. Oz has devoted other segments to the dangers of cosmetics-counter makeup (which he recommends you spray with disinfectant), tanning beds, shoes, nail salons, and that silent scourge: the mints you get next to the cash register in restaurants. Really, he did a whole big thing on these, and his grossed-out audience swore off them forever.

As if so many millions have been felled by free mints.

In Dr. Oz's world, pretty much anything that anyone else has ever touched, you shouldn't. He considers this common sense. I consider it obsessive-compulsive disorder. Since we're both alive and healthy, you can pick your camp.

Mine gets to keep eating free mints.

## Watch Out for Overheating!

Warning! "Hot weather can have a dire effect on senior health," reads the website Everyday Inflated Fears. Er, sorry—Everyday Health. So what are the symptoms of overheating? You'll never guess. Tops on the list: thirst! Then come those ever-so-subtle hints, including "staggering," "fainting," "high body temperature," and, in case you still didn't get the message, "coma."

My God, is there any way to avoid this stealthy danger? Thankfully, yes. Try these obscure but possibly helpful remedies: "Drink plenty of liquids." Also: "Avoid exercising in the heat." And: "Cover windows that are in direct sunlight." Do you think?

Not that I ever want to see seniors suffer from overheating, but I also don't want to see seniors suffer from being treated as if they've got bingo chips for brains. Anyone who's been around for sixty or more years has probably figured out by now that when you're thirsty, you should drink, and when you're staggering, it's time to take a break. Same goes for when you're in a coma.

## Watch Out for Musical Instruments!

"You don't want your child to live in a bubble . . . but remember that the more chances you take, the more likely your child will be injured or killed by an accident," reads the passive-aggressive Hidden Dangers to Your Child's Safety page on about.com.

And so it warns about the "hidden dangers" of bouncy houses and parade floats ("which can run over a child along the parade route") and my favorite new fear, "musical instruments, such as a guitar, that can hurt a young child who is playing with the string . . . if one of the strings that is under high tension breaks, flying into his eye, or scratches his face."

Forget the terrible grammar.

To me, that is the gold standard of warnings: a warning about an item that has been around almost forever and never been associated with any danger except to the eardrums of parents and music teachers. And now it's a bona fide health hazard! To come up with not just one but two possible injuries from a guitar takes warning genius. My hat is off to you, basic child–safety writers. (I just hope it doesn't accidentally hit you in the eye and scratch your cornea, possibly causing blindness.)

## Watch Out for Weather!

Have you noticed that when a big storm is coming up, it's no longer just a storm; it is "Winter Storm '07!" or "Heat Wave '10!" Jack Glass has. He's a scientist and an expert on disaster communication, and he has been watching weather "creep" for the past five years or so. "Now everything has a year after it," says Glass. The not-so-hidden message? This is it! The biggie! The one you'll always remember! "So everybody is out buying their milk, bread, and eggs, and suddenly it comes and goes with absolutely no impact."

But at least you've got food in the house.

## Watch Out for Warnings That Sound as if They Were Written by Lawyers on Crack!

T-Mobile put out a set of instructions for its customers, encouraging them to "use your phone in a safe and sensible manner." One of these "sensible" tips? "If your device rings and you discover it's in the backseat, do not crawl over the seat to answer it while driving."

That's verbatim. And it pretty much illustrates the whole problem. We get so many warnings flying at us that real dangers (drunk driving) and the almost hallucinatory ones (backseat-climbing driving) get jumbled together. What's really going to kill us? A kamikaze float? Winter Storm '11? Or sitting in the La-Z-Boy watching the news and overdosing on Doritos?

The fact is, the more strange and striking the warning, the less likely it is to be true, says David Freedman, author of *Wrong: Why Experts Keep Failing Us—And How to Know When Not to Trust Them.* We viewers tune in to the shocking studies because for some strange reason, we like to be scared. As kids, we had ghost stories. As adults, we have health stories. Either way, we listen up because something that seemed so innocent is about to kill us! But shouldn't it have killed us already? If the world is full of such horrible ills, why are we living longer than ever?

Turns out, we live in very safe times. Not perfectly safe; nothing is. But safe enough that instead of worrying about diphtheria, we're worrying about dip.

> "Instead of worrying about diphtheria, we're worrying about dip."

Pay attention to your health—and a little less to the health scare of the day—and you'll be fine. Provided, that is, you watch out for that onion dip, and the shopping carts, and your kid's Polly Pockets, and Fall Foliage Color-palooza '10, and the top button on your shirt, and . . .

# Humorist Jimmy Tingle Proposes an Alternative to the Alternative to the Alternative Energy Plan

BY JIMMY TINGLE

**There are more than two million people in this country currently serving time. For exercise, they lift weights all day. They get angrier and more frustrated, angrier and more frustrated, angrier and more frustrated. And when they're released, they are angrier and more frustrated . . . and bigger. We don't want them just getting bigger; we also want them to give back to society.**

As part of my comprehensive alternative-energy package, I am suggesting that every prison cell in the United States be equipped with an exercise bike, hooked up to a generator, generating electricity, with a very long cord going to the home of the prisoner's victim to help him out with his electric bill.

We could have another long cord going to the local public school, hooked up to a video screen showing the guy in his prison cell on an exercise bike, as a deterrent, like a modern *Scared Straight!*, only this would be called *Bored Straight*.

If pedaling is good for prisoners, I say it's good enough for us, too, especially if it'll improve the environment. Here's my idea: Forget hybrids and electrics. Why can't Detroit build cars that we pedal? Like the Flintstones?

I would pedal, my wife would pedal—even my thirteen-year-old son could pedal.

"But, Dad, I'm tired."

"Quiet. I'm taking you to soccer. The least you can do is pedal."

Cars that we pedal would help combat obesity, get us in shape, tighten up our abs, tighten up our butts, and bring back something that has been missing from American culture for at least thirty years: hitchhiking. No one picks up hitchhikers anymore. On your way home from work this week, if you see some big biker-looking dude with long hair and a leather jacket by the side of the road hitchhiking, you're probably not going to pick him up. However, if you needed someone to help you pedal . . .

"Excuse me. Are you a Hells Angel?"

"Why, yes, I am."

"Get in! Help me get this up to thirty-five."

We can also learn from other countries. In China, people used to pull their compatriots through the streets in little cart-like chariots called rickshaws. When I suggest the rickshaw as a means of transportation here, people look at me as if I am crazy.

"Jim!" they say. "Where are we going to find Americans to run through the streets pulling other Americans?"

Simple . . . joggers!

How many times has a person come up to you and said, "I jogged nine miles today!" Good. Pull somebody with you.

My brother Gary has run twenty-four Boston Marathons. Why can't he pull our mother to the supermarket? He could drop her off, run ten miles, come back, and pull her home. He could build lower- and upper-body strength while spending quality time with the family.

My friends, what I'm trying to say is, the solution to all our energy needs lies in tapping into America's historic can-do spirit with creativity, innovation, and optimism—even in the midst of disaster.

Eight days after the Gulf of Mexico sprang a leak, the federal government gave its approval to build a wind farm off Cape Cod. The bad news: It took nine years to get that approval.

Nine years to get approval to build a wind farm? This is America; there are many windy places. Why can't we put some of the windmills in the breakdown lane on the highway? Look at all that untapped wind!

Think about it: using wind, created by cars running on foreign oil, to engage windmills, to generate electricity, to reduce our dependency on foreign oil!

And that's not all.

I suggest that every traffic light in America be equipped with a little windmill to generate the power to run the traffic lights.

Of course, the naysayers attack my idea. "But Jim, what happens if one day the wind doesn't blow?"

Easy. You don't stop!

Do you know how much gasoline we waste waiting for the lights to change?

"But Jim, shouldn't we encourage people to take mass transportation?"

Sure, but there's one huge drawback to public transportation: Cars are more comfortable than subways. If the average American had his choice of going anywhere, do you think he would choose driving a car or standing in a moving cylinder chugging through the pitch-blackness of a tunnel built in 1901, while holding on to a metal pipe that one million people grabbed that morning, as he tries to balance himself between a homeless person, a bicycle, a baby carriage, and a folksinger? People banging into him, asking for money, crying for a bottle, singing a ballad . . . Of course, the average person will choose the car.

Therefore, we need to start building trains that are as private and as comfortable as our automobiles. We have to start building trains . . . of automobiles.

Detroit has seven million cars lying around not doing anything. I say string those babies together.

Imagine it: You go down into a subway station and a train of automobiles pulls up—nine hundred automobiles all attached bumper to bumper. Americans could have the privacy of an automobile in the realm of public transportation.

> "Detroit has seven million cars lying around not doing anything. I say string those babies together."

You could sit there on your way to work and listen to the radio, talk on a cell phone, drink a cup of coffee, read the paper, put on your makeup, and text your friends all at the same time . . . just like driving.

See? Saving energy is easy, and it won't affect our life-style one bit.

# The Mad Men of Pranks Inc.!

BY LANCE CONTRUCCI

**Walk into Jerry Stepani's office and you'll see vestiges of the practical jokes of yore. There's a whoopee cushion on the couch, a dollar tied to a string on the floor, even fake vomit on his desk.**

But Stepani, president of Pranks Inc., a subsidiary of Bloomberg, isn't looking back. The golden age of pranks is here. "There are big bucks in yucks," he says as he jolts me with a joy buzzer.

Stepani and company are busy establishing the U.S. Prank Exchange, which lets investors buy and sell shares in hoaxes. According to an article in the *Wall Street Journal*, "blue-chip pranks, like those involving whoopee cushions, are expected to have moderate growth, whereas tech and online pranks are expected to be highly volatile but . . ."

Okay, we're lying. There is no Pranks Inc., no Prank Exchange, no *Wall Street Journal* article, not even a Jerry Stepani, as far as we know. Too bad—we could make a mint, what with all the pranks being perpetrated on an unsuspecting public. Just last year, the world was introduced to bottled organic air (courtesy of Whole Foods Market), animal gyms (Virgin), and a new breed of sheep-sporting tartan-patterned wool (the *Daily Mail*), to name but a few. Bears may have decimated the stock and housing markets, but there's still a lot of bull in the bull business. Here, four of the best pranksters tell us what makes them trick.

## Gag Reflex

Forty-two-year-old comedian Tom Mabe was a prank prodigy, having executed his first when he was only eight. He had just made a snowman on the front lawn of his Louisville, Kentucky, home when he watched helplessly as teenagers in a car ran over it. He made another, with the same result. The third snowman he built was on a fire hydrant. "There I was with their wrecked car and water gushing out everywhere, and I acted like, "Gee, I didn't think anyone would hit it with his car," he says. "I had to do something. I was just a little guy. So I came up with this kind of cowardly way of getting revenge."

Mabe grew up to be six feet four inches tall, but he never lost the little-guy attitude. His specialty is torturing telemarketers. He once checked into a Washington, DC, hotel that was hosting a telemarketing convention and spent the night making phony phone calls, trying to sell the sellers insomnia medicine at three o'clock in the morning. The front desk manager finally begged him to stop because one of the guests was so outraged. Mabe promised to fix the situation. He phoned the guest and identified himself as the manager. "Sir, I'm sorry about your losing sleep," he said. "I believe we can make it up to you."

"Thank God," the man said.

"Here it is . . . *Rock-a-bye, baby, in the treetop . . .*"

**Why do you pull pranks?** "Revenge and fun. If some sales-man is going to call my house, it's game on."

**Best gag you've pulled off**: "One time there were a couple of homeless guys in front of a McDonald's. I called the restaurant impersonating a policeman and pretended that the men were actually undercover cops. I persuaded the manager to bring them burgers and coffee."

**Best gag someone else pulled off**: "My buddy Jim Clark

took his family to the zoo, and upon exiting, he and his family ran past the people entering screaming, 'Run, run! It's right behind us!' People were taking cover, jumping up on picnic tables!"

**Any pranks you regret pulling?** "I once saw a dead deer by the side of the road. I ran back to my house, put on a Santa suit, and then I lay down beside the deer—just in time for a school bus to drive by. Freaked the kids right out."

**Pearls of wisdom:** "If you're a revenge prankster like me, remember: Not everyone is evil, not even telemarketers. Every year around Christmas, when one of them calls, I'll always say something like, 'Hmmm, that transmission insurance policy sounds like something I could really use, but it's kind of expensive, and it is Christmas. Hmmm . . . Do you think if I put my kid on the phone, you could pretend to be Santa Claus and tell him you're not coming this year?' So far, no one has taken me up on this. Score one for humanity."

## Sir Pranksalot

Sir John Hargrave got into the pranks business honestly: He was born on April 1. With that head start, he founded one of the premier prankster sites on the web, zug.com, which stands for "zug is utterly great." The forty-one-year-old embarked on world hoax domination some years ago when, posing as a ten-year-old, he wrote to every U.S. senator asking them to send him a joke as part of a homework assignment. Many senators responded, including Maryland's Barbara Mikulski, who contributed this: "Why didn't the skeleton cross the road? Because he didn't have any guts!"

By the way, don't let Hargrave's lofty title fool you. He's from Boston. He added "sir" to his legal name when Buckingham Palace refused to knight him for "honourable pranking."

**Why do you pull pranks?** "It's a sport for thrill seekers. The moment before you pull off something, it's pure adrenaline."

**Best gag you've pulled off:** "I once filled out my tax forms using Roman numerals. The IRS was not amused."

**Best gag someone else pulled off:** "Mat Benote, a graffiti artist, hung one of his paintings at the Brooklyn Museum in New York. It took two days before they realized it didn't belong."

**Any pranks you regret pulling?** "No, but I do regret having been punked myself. Before my book *Mischief Maker's Manual* was published, I solicited celebrity blurbs on my website. I got an e-mail from a kid who said Eric Idle of Monty Python was his uncle. So the next

> "I once filled out my tax forms using Roman numerals. The IRS was not amused."

thing I know, I was e-mailing with Eric Idle, and having conversations with his assistant. A year later, I saw this article, 'How I Pranked John Hargrave.' It was the kid—he played all the parts in the prank: Eric Idle, the assistant, everyone."

**A gag anyone can pull off:** "Stick someone's toothbrush in a Dixie cup of water, and put it in the freezer overnight. Put it back in its normal place in the morning."

**Pearls of wisdom:** "Pranks and practical jokes should never be confused. A practical joke is something you pull on coworkers, like the guys in Utah who transformed their vacationing colleague's cubicle into a small cottage, complete with a working doorbell, mailbox, and ceiling fan. A prank goes after the man. For example, there's a video where Tom Cruise is being interviewed. The interviewer is holding a trick microphone and squirts water in Cruise's face. Cruise starts chewing him out, and we crack up because, well, Tom Cruise is the man."

## Getting Schooled

Tension fills the halls of collegehumor.com. Two of the humor site's writers are at war, a prank war to be precise. The small-scale gags that Streeter Seidell and Amir Blumenfeld first pulled on each other have ballooned into elaborate productions.

In one, Blumenfeld arranged for Seidell and his girlfriend to go to a Yankees game. Unbeknownst to Seidell, Blumenfeld also arranged for the scoreboard to display a bogus wedding proposal. A hidden camera recorded the couple's reaction. It's painful to watch. Seidell's girlfriend is understandably startled. Seidell is even more startled when she accepts. "I did not put that up!" he exclaims. "I don't want to marry you." She slaps him and leaves. For good. Seidell, age twenty-seven, says his friendly war with Amir has only escalated since then.

**Why do you pull pranks?** "It began as a fun way to kill boredom. Now I'm just trying to top the one before."

**Best gag you've pulled off:** "I arranged for Amir to be selected to take a halftime half-court shot for a half million dollars at a college basketball game. While Amir was led to a secluded office 'to sign forms,' I let the crowd in on the gag and requested their help. When Amir came back, we blindfolded him, and he took his shot . . . missing by at least twenty feet. But on cue, the crowd went crazy, as if he sank the shot. Amir did a victory lap around the court, yelling and punching the air. It lasted right up to the presentation of the fake check . . . which was presented by me. That's when he realized he'd been had."

**Best gag someone else pulled off:** "The lottery ticket

prank. It's done a lot, and for good reason. Videotape a lottery drawing. The next day, buy a ticket, asking for the same numbers that won the day before. Give that ticket to a friend and watch the 'live' drawing together. When he 'wins,' he will leap for joy like Amir did . . . until you turn off the tape."

**A gag anyone can pull off:** "Bet someone that you can make it so they cannot lift a glass of beer off the table with their thumbs. When they've agreed to the bet, have them place their thumbs on the table next to each other. Now balance the full glass of beer on their thumbs. Unless they want to take a beer bath, they're stuck."

**Pearls of wisdom:** "You need a bit of meanness to be funny, but too much and you make people uncomfortable." Like what Amir did to your ex-girlfriend? "Yeah."

## Prank You Very Much

On a freezing January morning, New York City commuters boarded subways from various lines and braced themselves for the day. They could not have expected this: Fellow passengers—businesspeople and college kids alike— removed their pants and skirts and nonchalantly rode to their destination, Union Square, in their underwear. Riders gawked, leered, and laughed their heads off. The 11th annual No Pants Subway Ride was another successful gag perpetrated by Charlie Todd and his New York prank collective, Improv Everywhere.

Todd has a curiously upbeat mission for a guy trying to pull a fast one on the populace: "Cause scenes of chaos and joy in public places." They stage such scenes about ten times a year. There was the impromptu wedding reception for an unsuspecting couple getting married at City Hall and Frozen Grand Central, in which two hundred "agents" (the preferred term for participants) milled about Grand Central Terminal's Main Concourse before unexpectedly freezing in place during rush hour.

Todd, age thirty-one, grew up in Columbia, South Carolina, and moved to New York City in 2001. It was there, in an East Village bar, that something changed his life for good—he pretended to be the alternative rock singer Ben Folds. "People were posing for photographs with me, the bartender gave me free drinks, a girl gave me her number," he says. "But what I liked about it was that it was a positive experience for everybody, even though they were being fooled. When it was over, I didn't smirk 'ha-ha, you've been pranked.' I just thanked everyone and left. It gave them something they could tell their friends. Even if they googled Ben Folds and found out he's, like, ten years older than me, they'd still have a wonderful story: 'This guy, for some reason, pretended to be Ben Folds!'"

> Todd has a curiously upbeat mission for a guy trying to pull a fast one on the populace: "Cause scenes of chaos and joy in public places."

**Why do you pull pranks?** "I get excited about pulling pranks that make people smile."

**Best gag you've pulled off:** "The fake U2 concert in 2005. We assembled a group of musicians—with me dressed as Bono—and played a rooftop concert in New York. It was a crazy twenty minutes for the crowd watching . . . especially when the police arrested us for unreasonable noise."

**Best gag someone else pulled off:** "Rob Cockerham posted a fake T.G.I. Friday's menu page on his website cockeyed.com and encouraged people to insert it inside a real T.G.I. Friday menu. It parodied the Atkins Diet and

We Have Other Funny People*

had really disgusting stuff, like Bacon Churner with Faux-tatoes: two whole sticks of fresh Dutch dairy butter on a bed of crisp bacon."

**A gag anyone can pull off:** "Here's one my college room-mates pulled on me: They covered every object and surface in my bedroom with tin foil. All the windows and light bulbs were blacked out. I needed a flashlight to even figure out what was going on."

**Pearls of wisdom:** "Anyone can pull pranks. Look at Frozen Grand Central. All you have to do is freeze in place."

# What Does a Movie Producer Do?

BY MATTY SIMMONS

## What does a producer do?

The screenwriter, obviously, writes the screenplay. The actors, of course, act in that screenplay. And the director, without question, directs the whole thing.

But what does the producer do?

I will attempt to explain.

A film producer is the guy who, when a writer tells him about a good idea he's got for a screenplay, says, "That was done in 1938 by William Wyler. It costarred Fredric March and Loretta Young, with Claude Rains playing the black hat. But you know what? I think we could update it, if instead of making the leading lady a nun, we have her working in a casino in Nevada. We put George Clooney in the Fredric March role, and we make him an undercover agent for the CIA who has tracked a Russian agent to Las Vegas. Angelina Jolie would be great for the girl.

"They meet and fall in love, but he discovers that she's pregnant by the Russian agent. George has been licensed to kill this guy, who, incidentally, will be played by Jack Black, but Angelina begs George not to kill the father of her unborn child. In a tearstained scene at the Las Vegas airport, Angelina says good-bye to George and walks to the plane to join Jack Black for the trip back to Moscow. Our big ballad here. Maybe we get Elton John.

"George stops at the airport and pulls out a quarter she gave him. He drops it in a slot machine. The place goes nuts—bells ringing and all that stuff. George has hit the

$1 million jackpot! He collects his money in a single large suitcase. It's all in ones, to make it more visual—this is a visual medium.

"He goes back to his hotel. He's still sick about losing Angelina. He takes the $1 million down to the hotel casino and puts the whole thing on number twenty-seven, which was their number. We see the ball rolling around and around and around endlessly, while the theme music, sung by Christina Aguilera, soars until every butt in every seat is up in the air. The ball drops into number twenty-nine, then hiccups slightly and pops into twenty-eight, then, as Christina reaches a pitch so high that every dog within a mile of any movie house in America is howling with pain, the ball goes blip—and drops into twenty-seven."

By now, the writer, who is on the edge of his seat listening to the producer, is ecstatic. "And Angelina returns to him!" he screams.

"No," says the producer. "That's what would have happened in 1938. Instead we go for total realism. George meets two bimbos, played by Lindsay Lohan and Kim Kardashian, buys champagne for everybody in Las Vegas, and sends a telegram to Angelina, which she gets as she and Jack Black land in Moscow. It reads simply '#*%! you!' in Russian.

"As we go out on a big rock number by Bon Jovi, George is buying a bra with diamond studs on it for Kim, and Lindsay gets the last big laugh of the movie by falling up a down escalator."

"I love it!" says the writer, leaping from his seat. He drives like a maniac back home and writes a first draft overnight, and the producer takes it to one of the studios.

There, a reader who occupies a small closet-like office in a building near the parking lot and drinks from a *Star*

*Wars* mug reads it and condenses it to about a page and a half. Finally, because this is a prestigious producer, it wends its way through numerous assistants and production vice presidents, and, on the big day, the producer arrives to meet the head of the studio.

The headman, who hasn't read the screenplay or the condensed version but does know who has been suggested for the leading roles, because that's more important than the script, says, "Hugh Jackman is in the dumper. Angelina's fine, and the kids like Jack Black. We want Brad Pitt for the guy and Ashton Kutcher for the girl's kid brother."

The producer doesn't remember that there is a kid brother, but he's on a roll, so why argue? He agrees to the casting.

"And," says the head of the studio, "we want Steven Spielberg to direct. We've already contacted him, and he says as long as you stay off the set, he'll do it."

The producer then negotiates his own deal, taking an exceedingly large piece of the pie, flies to Bimini, where his yacht has been moored for the winter, and for the next six months sails around the Greek islands with Britney Spears and her mother.

The picture is made and released, is a huge hit, and garners no Oscar nominations. The producer makes millions, leaves his yacht in Greece, flies back to America, and buys another one.

That's what a producer does.

At least, that's what I'm told.

# Make It Stop!!

**Know what grates on my nerves? Grown adults using the word "awesome" for every occasion.**

"Uncle Louie survived a heart attack."

"Awesome!"

"Uncle Louie cut his toenails."

"Awesome!"

When did this word come to dominate the English language alongside such stalwarts as *and*, *the*, *but*, and *fracking*?

Of course, sharing pet peeves is more fun than keeping them to ourselves. So to that end, I've called on a few fellow curmudgeons to drive a stake through the heart of our more loathsome fads. These novelists, business owners, humorists, and even our own magazine readers cover the gamut of peeved to pissed off. But they all have one thing in common . . . they're awesome!

## Technology

### AN INTIMATE KNOWLEDGE OF SOMEONE ELSE'S MULTIPLE E-MAIL ACCOUNTS

Now that people have several e-mail addresses, they expect you to keep track of them all. "Oh, you sent that to my AOL account? But I only check that on alternate Sundays. You should have sent it to my Mac e-mail or my Gmail. No wonder I didn't get back to you." This is even more maddening when all you've done is replied to the address from which the e-mail was sent!

—WILL SCHWALBE, EDITOR OF THINKBEFOREYOUSEND.COM

## CALLER ID

Technology is ruining everything. In particular, it's gotten rid of the unexpected call from out of the blue. You know what I'm talking about, right? You're in a horrible mood; the telephone rings. You don't know whether to pick it up. You're imagining it's that stupid Elizabeth person who always calls you because she is so bored at her job and wants you to entertain her, so you almost don't pick it up. But you do. And it's a stranger telling you something that totally changes your mood, your day, maybe your life.

My God, the total exciting transformation of the call from out of the blue. There is so little magic in adult life. This was one of the few true magical things that could happen to you. But now with caller ID and e-mails and texts, you know exactly who is trying to contact you and what he or she wants. And most tragically, there is no unfamiliar voice at the other end who says your name with a questioning tone. Maybe this never happened to you. But there was always the chance that it could.

—BRUCE ERIC KAPLAN WROTE FOR *SEINFELD*, AND PUT OUT A BOOK
OF CARTOONS CALLED *I LOVE YOU, I HATE YOU, I'M HUNGRY*

## TECHNOLOGY THAT'S TOO SMART FOR MY OWN GOOD

Message to iTunes: Okay, my recent nostalgia for the '70s got the best of me, and I downloaded a Dan Fogelberg song or two. Now my suggested download list is wearing a fringed coat and sporting sideburns that could keep a small family warm. I really don't want Bread's Greatest Hits or rare Jim Croce outtakes. It's as if my purchases of Green Day and the Arctic Monkeys were erased from your memory. Please, my trip to the '70s was supposed to be a brief visit, not a never-ending journey into the mellow.

—ANDREW ALEXANDER, EXECUTIVE PRODUCER
OF THE SECOND CITY COMEDY THEATER

We Have Other Funny People*

## Jargon

### "JUST SAYIN'"

They're two little words innocuous enough on their own, though together they are poison. *Just sayin'* is the Hummel Lil' Rascal of figures of speech, harmless until you look closer and see the slingshot in his back pocket. The way it's used is in the form of a pulled punch. "No one above the age of seven should be seen chewing gum. Just sayin'." "My boss smells like a brewery. Just sayin'." It's like a coy kicking of the dirt. "I'm going to say something offensive, but by adding these two words, I won't have to take responsibility for it." —JULIE KLAM, AUTHOR OF *YOU HAD ME AT WOOF*

### "SOME LOVE"

Where's the love? Lately, everywhere: "Vegan Diets Get Some Love." "Historic Windows Get Some Love."

*Love* preceded by *some* doth not always run smooth: "I have to quit being so teed off before I give him some love," a fan wrote of former Arizona Cardinals wide receiver Anquan Boldin. And we're all being told to love on demand: "Call Henry Waxman's office and give him some love!" Sorry, I don't know the congressman well enough. When love is reduced to little more than a verbal thumbs-up, I'll settle for some like.

—LESLIE SAVAN, AUTHOR OF *SLAM DUNKS AND NO-BRAINERS*

## Parenting

### YOONEEK BABY NAMES

I'm talking to you, Madysyn, and you, Aadinn, and you, too, Makayla. Or rather, your parents. This effort to be more kre8tiv by taking a perfectly okay name and contorting it with extra letters and strange substitutes only condemns your poor child to a lifetime of respelling her name, explaining its derivation, and assuring people that, yes, her parents really do in most cases know how to spell.

Most annoying of all, these bizarre spellings don't do anything to change the name's pronunciation or special-ness, so Madysyn in the end is really just plain old Madison. So why change the spelling in the first place? That's right: just to be annoying.

—PAMELA REDMOND SATRAN, COAUTHOR OF *THE BABY NAME BIBLE*

## Food and Drink
### SERVICE WITH A DOLLOP OF AIR

Why are restaurant menus enumerating the pedigree of every ingredient in a dish, as well as its preparation method, infused with a few ultra-foodie terms just in case you weren't confused enough?

You won't see broiled pork chops on a menu. Instead, it's Organic Heritage Pennsylvania Center-Cut Pork Loin Chop Broiled à la Plancha with a Soubise of Toy Box Tomatoes, Hydroponic Watercress, Micro Arugula, accompanied by a Nougatine of Spring Onions, garnished with a Daikon Escabèche, topped with Prune Essence and Juniper Foam. Want fries with that?

—KATIE WORKMAN, EDITOR IN CHIEF OF COOKSTR.COM

### IT'S BACON!

Don't you think bacon is a little too pleased with itself these days? This breakfast food, which began life humbly on the belly of a pig, has lately made its uppity way into all sorts of products. There's bacon air freshener, bacon mints, bacon beer, gummy bacon, bacon lip balm, bacon-flavored enve-lopes, bacon soap, bacon lollipops, bacon gum balls, bacon mayonnaise, bacon popcorn, bacon chocolate, maple bacon coffee. And should any of the above get stuck in your teeth, you can clean it out with bacon-flavored floss.

Actually, it's not bacon I hate. I hate the people who tell me, bursting with naughty pride, how they gobble up their favorite source of saturated fat by the pound. Big deal—so you're not a health foodie. Want to truly impress me with your reckless daring? How about trying a headcheese smoothie?

> ## Don't you think bacon is a little too pleased with itself these days?

—PATRICIA MARX, AUTHOR OF *HIM HER HIM AGAIN: THE END OF HIM*

## Media
### TELEVISION BANNER ADS

As a TV writer, I almost never watch TV. And one reason is those big banner ads that scroll across the bottom of the screen, interrupting a show I want to see to promote a show I never want to see. If I'm watching something about Charlemagne, do I need to know about an all-new season of *American Chopper*?

These banner ads cover up subtitles in foreign films and obscure key clues on mystery shows. And once, during the somber classic film *Saving Private Ryan*, a Day-Glo green banner unfurled featuring the capering cast of *Uncle Fatso's Family*. And I wondered, *Who are you people? And what are you doing in Occupied France?*

—MIKE REISS, A FOUNDING WRITER OF *THE SIMPSONS*

## Manners
### "SHOULD I FLUSH?"

It boggles my mind that anyone thinks it's okay to talk on a cell phone in a public restroom. Standing next to a man who is talking while conducting his business on and off the phone is disconcerting enough and invites the question, "Do I flush?"

But can you imagine being on the other end of the call? Don't make them ask, "Where are you?" Avoid the unpleasantness: Table your talk until far from the toilet.

—PETER POST, DIRECTOR OF THE EMILY POST INSTITUTE

## "HUH?"

We've changed the motto of the United States.

"Huh?" you say.

And you're right. "Huh?" is the nation's new rallying cry. Ladies say "huh?" Gentlemen say "huh?" Children say "huh?" to everything. You could tell my children that their Crocs are on fire and they'd say, "Huh?"

Once it would have been "pardon me" or "come again" or "sorry, Daddy, I didn't hear what you said." Now it's the dull, uncouth, distracted "huh?" This is the result of the dull, uncouth distractions of modern life. People are constantly staring at something other than the person speaking to them—a laptop, BlackBerry, video game, Kindle, text message—and wearing iPod earbuds and talking on a cell phone, too. The cell phone conversation goes like this: Person with cell phone pauses slack-jawed, says, "Huh?" and then pauses while something is said again. He now says something, waits for the corresponding "huh?" and repeats himself.

In 1956, Congress changed the motto of the United States to "In God We Trust" because nobody knew what the old motto meant anymore. America's original motto, appearing on the Great Seal of the United States since 1782, was "e pluribus unum" ("one out of many") or, as we might say today, "e pluribus huh?"

—P. J. O'ROURKE, AUTHOR OF *DON'T VOTE—
IT JUST ENCOURAGES THE BASTARDS*

# Relationships

## E-LATIONSHIPS

I'm going to do it this time: I'm breaking up with "e-lationships," those text/e-mail/instant messaging–only relationships. The last guy I connected with online seemed promising. He sent me several lengthy e-mails and then asked for my phone number. All good. Until the texting started.

In short order, he cycled through infatuation, obsession, jealousy, and annoyance . . . without ever talking to me on the phone! Needless to say, not a match.com made in heaven.

—JENNIFER WORICK, COAUTHOR OF *THE WORST-CASE SCENARIO SURVIVAL HANDBOOK: DATING AND SEX*

## TOO MANY KODAK MOMENTS

There's nothing wrong with sharing photos of your children with family and friends. But must you send all five hundred in your memory card? Remember the moral of *Jurassic Park*: Just because you're technologically able to do something doesn't mean it's a good idea.

—RAQUEL D'APICE, COMEDIAN

# Entertainment

## THE DEMISE OF THE LAUGH TRACK

Whatever happened to the sitcom laugh track? Sure, shows seem edgier without one, but not all of us are very good at guessing when to laugh. Watching a laugh-track-less sitcom these days is like trying to solve a mystery. You know there are clues; you just wish that one of them was the sound of prerecorded laughter.

—SHAP SWEENEY, CREATIVE DIRECTOR OF THE HUMOR WEBSITE COMEDYSMACK.COM

## THE SHAKY CAM

Some directors want to put us in the middle of the action by using fast-moving, handheld cameras. I got that. But it's literally making me sick. I get nauseated when cameras move so fast that the smackdowns in movies like *Batman Begins* and *Quantum of Solace* are just one big blur. If I really wanted to feel like I was in a fight, I'd go pick one.

—MATT ATCHITY, EDITOR OF ROTTENTOMATOES.COM, A FILM-REVIEW SITE

## PERSONAL SCREENS ON AIRPLANES

I love having a TV set embedded in the seat back in front of me during a long flight, but touch screens? With games that require a lot of tapping? Get seated in front of a gamer and it feels like your chair has a built-in woodpecker. Even someone who can't decide on a movie to watch can tap you into insanity on a long flight.

—DOUG LANSKY, AUTHOR OF *THE TITANIC AWARDS: CELEBRATING THE WORST OF TRAVEL*

## Ten Trends We'd Like to See

"Pull up your pants," "pay it forward," and please—please!—"put shopping carts back where they belong." I asked our readers what fads they would like to see take hold. Those topped the list. But they didn't stop there:

Say "you're welcome" instead of "no problem," which implies it might have been a problem.

—PATRICIA B., CHANNAHON, ILLINOIS

A universal hand signal for poor drivers that means, "Sorry, I'm an idiot." —LAURA M., ST. LOUIS, MISSOURI

We Have Other Funny People*

An understanding among voters that a negative political ad will disqualify that candidate. —DOUG M., TUPELO, MISSISSIPPI

Allow pro golfers to wear shorts in PGA tournaments.
—DAVID G., MOLINE, ILLINOIS

Subject-verb agreement.
—JUDY G., ATLANTA, GEORGIA

"A universal hand signal for poor drivers that means, 'sorry, I'm an idiot.'"

People getting along as well as dogs do at the dog park.
—BRYANT H., HUNTSVILLE, ALABAMA

More inviting, user-friendly porches.
—DR. BOB L., OGDENSBURG, NEW YORK

Less Facebook, more face time. Cherish the people, not their personal Internet accounts.
—MERCY S., BINGHAMTON, NEW YORK

People discussing topics other than sports and home renovations. Something—anything!—deeper than scores and drywall. —GINA B., JOPPA, MARYLAND

I just want my cat to stop stepping on my head while I'm trying to sleep. —EILEEN E., FIELDSBORO, NEW JERSEY

# PART FIVE

# I Suck Up to Famous People

# A Q&A with the King of Ha-Has, Andy Simmons

BY ANDY SIMMONS

**Andy Simmons:** I just want to say, Mr. Simmons, that we're huge fans of yours here at *Reader's Digest* and that you're much better looking in person than in print.

**Andy Simmons:** Thank you, Mr. Simmons.

**AS:** Looking back on your long, remarkable career, you've interviewed just about every important humorist there is. Did anyone ever say your questions were stupid?

**AS:** One: Don Rickles. It was right after he told me a story about how he and Dean Martin were sneaking drinks backstage at President Reagan's inaugural bash before going on, even after Frank Sinatra told them not to.

**AS:** Why did Rickles get upset?

**AS:** I asked him if the booze helped his performance. He responded by calling me a dummy, insisting my wife was an idiot for marrying me, and even threatened to come over to my house and smack me around. Getting insulted by Don Rickles? It doesn't get any better than that.

**AS:** Who was the nicest person?

**AS:** They're all nice. If not, I'll write something nasty about them. I'm very petty. But I will say that Bob Newhart was extremely pleasant. I interviewed him for our advice issue. The topic was how to be funnier. These were his three tips:

1. **Know thy audience.** "Your audience will tell you where to go. One time I happened to use the word *denigrate* onstage, and it didn't get any reaction. So as I continued my act, the left side of my brain was fast-forwarding to see if I had any other big words coming up."

2. **Follow the signposts.** "I used to do this routine: 'Let's be honest, guys. We've all done this—the wife's out of the house and the kids are gone, so you go into her dressing room and put on one of her gowns and walk around the house. We've all done that, right, guys?' And based on how soon they began to laugh, that told me what kind of audience I had."

3. **The world is weird—embrace it!** "I saw something in the paper that was so odd, it was hysterical: They assassinated the minister of tourism in Afghanistan. What threat did he represent? And how busy could he have been? A phone call every couple of months? A newlywed couple saying, 'We've argued about this long enough. Let's flip a coin—Paris or Kabul?'"

**AS:** Another sweetheart is Dolly Parton. She exudes sunshine, although she denies it.

> **Dolly Parton:** "People say to me, 'You always seem so happy. Are you really that happy?' I say, 'Hell no, nobody's that happy. That's Botox.'"

**AS:** You're recognized in the business for being pretty lazy. What was your easiest interview?

**AS:** Jerry Stiller and Ann Meara. I could have left the tape recorder going, gone to a Mets game, come back, and they'd still be talking over each other. Here's a snippet that was left out of our interview:

> **STILLER:** We decided [in the '70s] that being a Las Vegas act was getting tough mainly because we had two kids.
> **MEARA:** Amy and Ben.
> **STILLER:** What are you going to do? Put them in school in Vegas? You know what Vegas is today? You should have seen what it was then.
> **MEARA:** I think the Mormons have taken over or something.
> **STILLER:** No, it was not the Mormons. It was just that they cleaned up the town, and the prostitutes had to leave, and then . . .
> **MEARA:** Which is sad, because a lot of people came to Vegas for the prostitutes.
> **STILLER:** Not us.
> **MEARA:** Well, we don't know.
> **STILLER:** What do you mean, "We don't know?"

**AS:** I couldn't get a word in.

**AS:** Interviews are often done over lunch, so as to create a relaxed atmosphere. What was the best meal you ever got out of an interview?

**AS:** With out a doubt, the one with Robin Williams. We

were in a lovely restaurant in Toronto, where he was shooting a movie. If I remember correctly, Robin had salmon, a Caesar salad, and an ice tea, while I ordered a lovely Niçoise salad, featuring hearty chunks of tuna. Not the kind that comes out of a can, mind you. The kind that comes out of an ocean. Robin was great. He even offered to pick up the tab. But one thing kept gnawing at me throughout our chat: Those damn Niçoise olives. They're miniscule. Robin was going on about his life, his career, his addictions, his friendship with Christopher Reeve—all fascinating stuff. But all I could think of was, *Why can't they replace Niçoise olives with kalamata olives? Or those black, crinkly ones, what are they called? Better yet, why olives at all? Why not M&Ms? Everyone loves M&Ms. They're easy to eat, and they don't leave a mess on your hands.*

**AS:** Any megalomaniacs in the group?

**AS:** Yes, *Doonesbury* cartoonist Garry Trudeau. I asked him what he would do if he ruled the world.

> **GARRY TRUDEAU:** I'd ban reality shows. They're not humiliating enough. The "stars" never figure out how appalling they are. For instance, when Jersey Shore's The Situation looks in the mirror, he's obviously very pleased with what he sees. Whereas if I ever looked in the mirror and saw The Situation staring back, I'd have to kill myself.

**AS:** Any one ever bring you down?

**AS:** Aside from you? Joy Behar with a story about one of her first gigs.

I Suck Up to Famous People

**JOY BEHAR:** I was working the Catskills one time. The main speaker was an expert on the Holocaust—a brilliant, somber man. He ended his lecture by singing about the Holocaust. It was like one of those Jewish songs sung at funerals. There wasn't a dry eye in the place. When he finished, he left the stage to silence. Then the emcee came on stage to announce, "And now the comedy of Joy Behar!"

**AS:** The opposite of downer was Mindy Kaling, who plays the narcissist Kelly Kapoor on *The Office*. When I asked Mindy what Kelly would do if she'd replaced Michael Scott as the new boss of Dunder Mifflin, she replied:

**MINDY KALING:** Kelly's number one priority would be to make the office look like the inside of her favorite store at the mall, Anthropologie. She'd get Nate Berkus in there to empty it out, make all the furniture sleeker, put a big contrast wall in there. Kelly would fire people she deemed insignificant so she'd have more money to make the office look great. Creed is gone, Meredith is gone, Kevin is gone—anyone who she thinks makes the office look uncool. But she'd think of a reason for doing it. I mean, she's smart enough to know you can't fire someone for being uncool.

**AS:** Have you ever actually learned anything from the people you've interviewed?

**AS:** Yes, from Alan Alda. He told me that people don't like being cornered at parties—away from the interesting people, food, and drinks—and regaled with joke after awful joke by some dullard who doesn't know when to stop. Had you heard this rule before? About not boring people at parties? Jokes, it seems, are out; wit and charm are in. This was the single biggest party-going revelation I'd encountered since my friend Ratso taught me the art of situating myself near the kitchen so that I wouldn't get shut out from the hors d'oeuvres. Not being boring. I'm all over that!

> "He told me that people don't like being cornered at parties—away from the interesting people, food, and drinks."

**AS:** I find it odd that people who would otherwise go out of their way to ignore you actually take the time to answer your questions, many of which, as we've discussed, are not particularly clever.

**AS:** I know. Weird, right? And yet I've chatted with many of my favorite comedians, like Woody Allen, Lewis Black, Jerry Lewis, Richard Belzer, Carl Reiner, and Whitney Cummings, some of whom are represented here.

# Tragedy Tomorrow, Comedy Tonight: A Chat with Woody Allen

America's greatest living comic auteur can't understand why everyone thinks he's a bumbling schlemiel. Neurotic, maybe. But a schlemiel?

"I was always an exceptionally fine athlete, always the first chosen in any schoolyard game," insists Woody Allen. "I was popular in school. Always very successful. And so I never had any feelings of great schlemielism."

It's his slight build and thick, black-rimmed glasses that have betrayed him, he says, before applying this remarkable label to himself: "If there's such a thing as Joe Six-Pack, that's me. When I get home from work tonight, I'm not going to snap open Dostoyevsky. I'm going to get out a beer and watch the Yankees."

This, from a man who puts Schopenhauer number one on his list of funniest German philosophers. This from a man who can put Schopenhauer on any list.

Allen is undoubtedly a victim of his own success. He became famous playing roles like the abused product tester (abused by the products!) with the schlemielesque name Fielding Mellish in *Bananas*, who, when summoned by a South American dictator, arrives with a box of Danish pastries (because you never go empty-handed to someone's home). And in *Take the Money and Run*, he portrayed an inept bank robber who has trouble convincing the tellers he's serious, which might have lent some oomph to that perception, too.

Though he may be a beer-swilling Yankees fan, the fact is, Allen has never been just the guy next door. And his earliest recollections in comedy bear that out.

It was the mid-'50s and the twenty-year-old Allen had found the Holy Grail of humor-writing for Sid Caesar's *Caesar's Hour*. He'd be working alongside future legends Mel Brooks, Neil Simon, and Larry Gelbart. Although the writers were, to a man, mensches (Brooks, he says, was particularly "lovely to work with"), the crazed Caesar was intimidating.

One day Caesar summoned Allen and Gelbart to his house to work on a script. There, Caesar and Gelbart decided to indulge in a steam bath. Not Allen.

"I wouldn't take my clothes off. I just didn't feel right doing it," he says, horrified at the thought of appearing naked in front of his boss. "And you know, they thought I was the oddball. I mean, the two of them peel off their clothes at the drop of a hat and get into a steam bath, and I'm the oddball." He was sounding downright schlemielly before further explaining, "I was not a cigar-smoking, one-of-the-guys getting into steam baths. I was, you know, more fragile."

What Allen is is complex. Don't file him under "nut" and leave it at that; otherwise you'll miss out on the tangled genius that marks his work. He's one of the few filmmakers capable of delivering hysterical one-liners ("I don't want to achieve immortality through my work; I want to achieve immortality through not dying"), followed by a brilliant sight gag or a bit of inspired slapstick. He's the equivalent of the Beatles, trading ballads with hard rock.

Allen used this complexity to launch an incredibly successful film career on his own terms. Early on, he decided he would make the sort of movies he loved growing up.

"When I was a kid," he says, "I enjoyed sophisticated comedy, movies with Champagne corks popping and people dressing for dinner and talking on white telephones and making witty conversation. Or the Marx Brothers or W. C. Fields—you know, kind of a very high level of comedy."

Of course, he added some decidedly Woody Allen modifications to his flicks. Instead of a William Powell or a Myrna Loy, you'll meet characters who are "bright Upper East Side New Yorkers," he says, "who are in psychoanalysis and have difficulty with their interpersonal relationships."

Allen uses film to examine just how unfair life can be. In his movie *Vicky Cristina Barcelona* he has one of his characters say of his father, a poet who refuses to publish his work, "He affirms life in spite of everything."

"I am, unfortunately, not like that character. I'm like the squire in Bergman's *The Seventh Seal*," says Allen, of a servant who follows his knight to his death. "I go at the end, but under protest.

"Moral dilemmas are the same now as they were in the beginning of time. People are predatory and competitive," he says matter-of-factly. "The issues today may be global warming and Darfur, but it's the same thing. We still don't like each other. I always felt if the bigots got their way and they eliminated all the blacks and all the Jews, then they would turn on the next group of people and the next group. Finally, when there were just two people left on earth, the right-hander would turn on the left-hander."

Of course, the obvious question when discussing moral dilemmas with Woody Allen would be to raise his own, particularly the Woody/Mia/Soon-Yi fiasco. For those of you living in a monastery in the '90s, Soon-Yi was Mia Farrow's adopted daughter. Woody was Mia's beau. It got ugly quickly after the fifty-six-year-old Woody lit out with the twenty-one-year-old Soon-Yi. The two have been married for fifteen years and have two children.

I don't ask about it, though. It's lousy journalism, I know. But the topic has been played to death. And besides, I like the guy. He's as pleasant as can be, and his telltale New Yawkese has put me at ease. Besides, like most fans, even if I don't condone what he did, I can relate to his neurosis and his defiant "I'm no schlemiel" stance.

So instead I ask the only question that pops to mind: "Why are you so depressing?"

"I don't know. Maybe it's chemical," he says. "My mother said when I turned five, I turned gloomy."

How gloomy? One of his least favorite movies is the Frank Capra life-affirming tearjerker, *It's a Wonderful Life*.

"I think it's dopey," he says.

The movie, of course, is a shot of curare to a life-stinks kind of guy like Woody Allen.

> "My mother said when I turned five, I turned gloomy."

"So how would you remake it so it's not dopey?"

"I'd make it," he says, "where the guardian angel saves Jimmy Stewart's life on the bridge and Jimmy Stewart decides to become a serial killer."

"Why don't you just find God?" I ask Allen. "Wouldn't it make your life easier?"

Allen is a nonbeliever. He famously summed up his position this way: "To you, I'm an atheist; to God, I'm the loyal opposition."

"If you actually have faith, if you believe that there's more to life in a positive sense, then of course it's a wonderful, wonderful thing," he says.

But . . .

"I can't bring myself to do it. If I'm sitting next to a guy and he has true belief, I look at him and think, *Poor thing, you really are deluded.* But," he concedes, "his life is much better than mine."

What keeps Woody Allen from going over the brink is his work, one reason he has averaged a film a year over the past decade. Beyond film, he was able to direct a Puccini comedy for the Los Angeles Opera. "I got badgered into it," he whines. "I would rather coach the New York Knicks than direct the opera. . . . I think I could do a better job coaching the Knicks."

In the meantime, Allen keeps churning out more films. And the schlemiel/depressive/comic genius . . . whatever . . . sounds genuinely happy. His work relaxes him, he says. "It's like therapy for an inpatient in an institution."

# The Funniest Person I Know: Carl Reiner on Mel Brooks

**I've known Mel since 1950 when we both worked on *Your Show of Shows*. One day, I suggested we do a skit where we re-create the news.**

To prove it could work, I turned to Mel out of the blue and said, "Here's a man who was actually at the scene of the crucifixion two thousand years ago, isn't that true, sir?"

And he said, "Oh, boy."

"And you knew Jesus?"

"Oh, sure. Thin boy, used to come into the store, never bought anything. Used to come in with twelve other guys. All they ever asked for was water."

Now, Sid Caesar was the greatest sketch comic. He was a method actor and didn't know it. We were working on a skit using pickles. He's holding an imaginary jar and struggling to get the lid off. Finally, he opens it. But there was no laugh in it, and we said no, it didn't work. But as we moved on to something else, he pantomimed twisting the imaginary lid back on the imaginary jar and placed it down on an imaginary table. He wasn't even aware he was doing it.

But with Mel, I never knew what he would say. Once I asked the two-thousand-year-old man what's the difference between comedy and tragedy. He ad-libbed, "Tragedy is when I get a paper cut on my finger. Comedy is if you fall down an open manhole." I still see him almost every night, and if I'm bored, I just pose a question to the two-thousand-year-old man, and he never ceases to amaze me.

# Robin Williams Grows Up (Just a Little)

**Robin Williams likes to work without a net. If you've ever seen a recording of him onstage, you know what I mean. His shows are totally improvised: no canned jokes, no dress rehearsal, no repeating lines that worked the night before.**

His movies aren't a whole lot different. They may always start with a script, but where it goes after that is anyone's guess. Williams himself often doesn't have a clue. So as I awaited the comedian at a table in a Toronto restaurant, incessantly testing the batteries on my digital tape recorder, I was prepared to be greeted by Williams reciting the Gettysburg Address as James Brown or using a Croatian accent while performing a German slap dance. Instead, the man who took a seat opposite me was a subdued, normal guy—who happens to be abnormally funny.

**Andy Simmons:** You trained at Juilliard, a very serious acting school. When did you start concentrating on humor?

**Robin Williams:** I left school and couldn't find acting work, so I started going to clubs where you could do stand-up. I've always improvised, and stand-up was this great release. All of a sudden it was just me and the audience.

**AS:** What's that like, working in front of a live audience?

**RW:** It's frightening and exhilarating. It's like combat.

Look at the metaphors: You kill when it works; you die when it doesn't.

**AS:** You bomb.

**RW:** Bombing is bad. Killing is good.

**AS:** Do you remember your first routine?

**RW:** Vaguely. It was in San Francisco, in the '70s, at this place called The Committee. I was a football quarterback on acid—kind of a funky Lawrence Welk, like Welk doing *Soul Train*. It was a pretty wild time.

**AS:** There are different kinds of humorists—the political type like Jon Stewart, or the more observational kind like Jerry Seinfeld. How would you define your humor?

**RW:** It's kind of the lazy Susan effect. It has samples of all—blue, some very personal observations, some political observations, some world observations, some making fun of the celebrity world, and it's insanity and hype. It kind of goes everywhere.

**AS:** Do you work from a script?

**RW:** No. It's more like headlines. "German Pope." You build off a topic and explore how far you can go.

**AS:** Do you practice?

**RW:** No, I don't practice anything. I spend time looking over ideas and then just get out and do it. Even when I did

I Suck Up to Famous People

my Broadway show, I did fifteen minutes no one had seen before, because that was the night that Michael Jackson protested about Al Sharpton bailing on him. I said, "Wow, if that man bails on you, this must be really a lost cause."

**AS:** Wouldn't it be safer to script it?

**RW:** Safer is not a good thing.

**AS:** Do you ever self-censor?

**RW:** People would say I never censor. As Billy Crystal says, "I don't have that button."

**AS:** Is anything not funny to you?

**RW:** Anything that is not funny at a certain point will be funny.

**AS:** You've gotten away with stuff others wouldn't. Why?

**RW:** Maybe it's a likability, that I seem fluffy. Occasionally I will be angry—someone will really push the button. But I always came from the idea that I enjoy this. It's a blast. Maybe that keeps it from being intense.

**AS:** At this point do you consider yourself a comic first, then an actor, or vice versa?

**RW:** For me, they're interchangeable. They feed each other nicely. And comedy pays the bills if I can't find a film.

**AS:** You grew up outside Detroit, and your father, Robert, worked in the auto industry. What family vacations did you take?

**RW:** There weren't that many, because Dad was working so much. I remember going to New York once—I'd never been in the city—and the noises at night and looking out the window. You would hear everything, and those garbage trucks.

**AS:** Why do you now live in San Francisco as opposed to Hollywood or New York?

**RW:** My father retired to San Francisco, and I got a chance to know him and be around him. It's always been some-place where everything changed for the better. It's always been a home for me. And up to that point, I'd been at an all-boys private school. All of sudden I was in a coeduca-tional school. There were girls everywhere. They weren't brought in for dances and then taken away. And the first time I saw fog, I didn't know what it was. I thought it was poison gas. "What's that, Dad?"

**AS:** Tell us more about your father.

**RW:** He worked for Lincoln-Mercury when they made great cars. His job was to troubleshoot, to travel around to different dealerships, and eventually he saw the company's quality go downhill. They offered him loads of cash to stay, and he said no thanks. For me he's always been this very ethical guy.

**AS:** How does that show up in your life now?

**RW:** I have like a no-fly zone with doing commercial endorsements and product placements. That's a residual from Dad. I just want to do movies, and I want to sell them. I don't want to link up with some product.

**AS:** Lots of actors won't endorse products in America, but will do commercials in Japan. What do you think of that?

**RW:** Number one, financially, I don't have to do it. Number two, the people who do it, God bless them, but you think, *Why does he need to do that? He's got hundreds of millions of dollars.* Unless it's like Paul Newman with salad dressing, where the money goes to charity. If I could do something like that with a product, I would.

**AS:** I heard that you own a vineyard and produce wine in Napa Valley.

**RW:** I've owned the ranch for about twenty-six years, but I've only been growing grapes for the last fifteen.

**AS:** But you no longer drink, so how do you know if the wine is any good?

**RW:** The people running the ranch and my wife are all really knowledgeable.

**AS:** Why did you stop drinking?

**RW:** Because my first son was about to be born and I thought, *I can't continue this way.*

**AS:** Do you think you had a problem?

**RW:** The drinking was tied into cocaine. You needed to drink, especially hard liquor, to take the edge off the coke. So that would usually be this kind of hook for me.

**AS:** How crazy did you get?

**RW:** Not too crazy, but it was enough to go, *Uh-uh*. Especially with work. Hangovers don't make you a nice person.

**AS:** Was it easy for you to quit?

**RW:** It was kind of a decompression—from straight alcohol to mixed drinks to wine to spritzers—and then you're out.

**AS:** Tell us about your friendship with Christopher Reeve.

**RW:** At Juilliard, he lived nearby, and he literally fed me for a while. I'd go to his house and, as I say, borrow food. "Tuna, thank you." We were totally opposite—me coming from the West Coast and a junior college, and him from the hard-core Ivy League. He used to be the studly studly of all studlies, and I was the little fool ferret boy. It was astonishing to see that women just responded to him like [makes whooshing noises].

**AS:** After his accident, I was amazed at how strong he was.

**RW:** Yeah. I don't know how many times he had near-death experiences. When your spinal cord freezes up, you're vulnerable to everything. But he was tough as nails. And he kept a great, kind of dark sense of humor about it, but also was able to accomplish amazing things. Now, with the war, we have more and more people coming in with spinal injuries. What he got going—especially with stem cells—there's amazing potential there.

**AS:** You were involved with Comic Relief. Are there any other causes that are close to your heart?

**RW:** There's Chris [Reeve]'s paralysis foundation, and there's Lance [Armstrong]'s foundation connected with cancer survivorship.

**AS:** I understand you've cycled with Armstrong. What was that like?

**RW:** It's like lap-dancing with Angelina Jolie. The first five minutes are amazing, and then she takes off. It's like, "Bye-bye. Bye-bye."

**AS:** You've done several USO shows. Did you go to Iraq?

**RW:** I was in Iraq, Afghanistan, Djibouti, Bahrain. The first year I went pretty much by myself. Then I went with General [Richard] Myers, head of the Joint Chiefs of Staff. The shows and audiences were amazing. You'll never get a better group of people.

**AS:** Was it dangerous?

**RW:** Yeah, we were doing open-air shows in a place where we could get mortared. I did a show and said, "You're all wearing flak vests. I didn't get that memo." And leaving is kind of scary. They do combat takeoffs.
It's like a really intense roller coaster—straight up, at night, no lights. Everybody in the cockpit's wearing night-

vision goggles, and you're in the back in the dark. Then they level off at fifteen thousand [feet] because that's outside the range of shoulder-fired anti-aircraft missiles.

## "You're all wearing flak vests. I didn't get that memo."

**AS:** Then you try to find your stomach.

**RW:** Yeah, it's like, "Oh, there's my corn." "Excuse me, sir, would you hand me my sphincter?"

**AS:** You did some stand-up specials after 9/11.

**RW:** I did an event in Washington, and it was like we lifted a sea. If you remember immediately after [9/11], there was a stunned shock—kind of this feeling of "what do we do now?" I started performing, and there was a catharsis in the laughing. People started to be able to laugh again. Laughter can be many things—sometimes a medicine, sometimes a weapon, depending on who's administering it.

**AS:** Do you ever use humor as a weapon?

**RW:** Oh, big time. It's a great defense, and an offense, too. Usually the recipient isn't too happy about it, but the people around are laughing.

**AS:** But in this case the laughter really did have a healing power?

**RW:** Healing isn't the word. Therapeutic maybe, or cathartic. After being in extreme situations, it kind of brings you back to life.

# A Comic's World

When I began working on this piece about comedians' oddest and funniest professional moments, the first thing I did was to call Jerry Lewis's office.

"Is Jerry, there?" I bellowed into the phone. "This is Andy Simmons from *Reader's*—"

"Mr. Lewis is not in," his assistant interrupted. "Send a fax, and if he wants to talk to you he'll call you."

A fax? Who does that anymore? "Can't I e-mail? The e-mail is right here on my computer. I can stay seated. The fax is all the way down the hall in a dark, scary room, and I'm not sure how it works."

"Mr. Lewis doesn't do e-mail. You have to fax." *Click.*

I found the fax machine as I remembered it—alone in a shadowy corner, in a gloomy closet, next to a reel-to-reel recorder, an Edsel, and an old Mississippi paddle ship. I cleared away the cobwebs and fed the note into its open maw, making sure to remove my hand quickly before it, too, got faxed over to Jerry. The machine gulped down the paper whole, as if it were starving. "More, more, more!" I thought I heard it shout as I ran out the door.

As I walked back to my desk I had no idea whether this was going to work. A fax? What, his teletype wasn't working? Should I see if Samuel Morse could lend a hand? Maybe . . .

My phone rang.

"Is this Andy Simmons?" demanded the voice on the other end.

I groaned. I was sure it was that guy who'd been pestering

me to run some gags he took from 1960s era *Reader's Digest*. "You're stealing our jokes, which we stole from someone else!" I kept telling him, but he didn't care.

"Yes," I croaked.

"This is Jerry."

"Jerry who?"

"Jerry Lewis!"

Who knew fax machines still work?

We had a delightful chat, and I sat there howling as he regaled me with a story that had happened to him while filming *Cinderfella*.

Here, Jerry and thirteen other comics—some young, some old-school, some famous, some soon-to-be—share the funniest and oddest things to happen to them during their careers.

## I Almost Died Laughing

JERRY LEWIS IS A COMEDIAN, ACTOR, PRODUCER, WRITER, DIRECTOR, SINGER . . .

I'm preparing the big finale for my 1960 film *Cinderfella*. The setting is a ballroom. The centerpiece: a long, majestic staircase with sixty-four steps. I'd flown in the Count Basie Orchestra from New York, so the soundstage is packed with hundreds of crewmembers, actors, extras, musicians, and visitors. I tell the cameraman where to set up the camera and what his cue is. Now I'm ready to film. I make my entrance at the top of the stairs. The camera follows me as I do my choreographed routine, going from the top stair all the way into the ballroom. I go to my costar Anna Maria Alberghetti. I take her hand and kiss it. I leave her and run up those sixty-four stairs in nine seconds flat. Nine seconds flat!

And then I wind up at the hospital—I had a heart attack at the top of the stairs.

That's not the funny part.

The film and all those actors, extras, crewmembers, and musicians are on hold for eight weeks because I'm now inside an oxygen tent. We're talking 1960, so it's a huge, canvas-like affair—square, with zippers. And on the top of it, there's a flap you can open to put in the stethoscope, medicine, and so on.

That night, my father comes into my room. He opens the little flap on the oxygen tent, sticks his face inside, and says, "Do you know what you're doing to your mother?"

## My Successful Career

JUDAH FRIEDLANDER PLAYS FRANK ROSSITANO ON NBC'S *30 ROCK*.

People often ask me, "How did you get started in stand-up comedy?" I tell them, "I got drafted right out of high school." I was in tenth grade, about to turn twenty-four. In the middle of class, I decided to make fun of the teacher. Everyone started laughing. Students fell out of their chairs and were convulsing on the floor. Other classrooms emptied out and squeezed into our room. The principal entered to stop the chaos. But he laughed harder than anyone.

> "It got too crowded, so I karate-kicked the wall down and took the show outside to the parking lot."

It got too crowded, so I karate-kicked the wall down and took the show outside to the parking lot. The cops and military were there. Not for security, but because they really appreciate a quality comedy show.

Two hundred miles away, Jeff Bloomwichz, the top comedy scout in America, was driving his speedboat in the Atlantic Ocean. He followed the sound of earthshaking guffaws to my show. Afterward, Jeff stepped out of his speedboat and said, "Funny stuff, kid." I signed a deal to turn pro right there in the parking lot. The rest is history.

## Joan of Arch

WHITNEY CUMMINGS STARS IN NBC'S *WHITNEY.*

The way comics show love and admiration for one another is by insulting one another on the *Comedy Central Roast.* But the key to a roast working is that the roastee has to enjoy it, or else it feels mean. That's what happened when we roasted Joan Rivers.

Greg Giraldo went up first and ripped into her, but he got no reaction from her. The next comic went up, same thing. Everyone was laughing except Joan. The comics were getting nervous. We were whispering, "Her feelings are hurt. Look at her. She's not smiling!" I was panicking. Here she is, my hero, and I was convinced she would never speak to me again.

But Joan Rivers—the butt of all these nasty jokes—saved the day. Sensing the unease among the comics, half-way through the show she stood up and assured us, "I'm having fun. This is funny!" It turns out she was a victim of her Botox. She had to subtitle her own face so that people would know she was enjoying herself.

## My Favorite Act

DAN "LARRY THE CABLE GUY" WHITNEY IS
A STAND-UP COMEDIAN.

Johnny Vegas was a crazy Brit.

I remember he was standing on a table at this comedy club belting out "God Bless America" when suddenly he fell off and cracked his head open. The place went silent. Is he dead? Is he alive? No one knew. Then out of the blue, a voice shouted, "Come on, you sorry so-and-sos, sing with me!" Johnny staggered to his feet and, with blood pouring from his head, marched around the club, leading us all in a sing-along. I'm telling ya, the Brits do some strange stuff.

## Hanging Out with Royalty

DON RICKLES IS, WELL, DON RICKLES.

About fifty years ago, I'm sitting in the lounge at the Sands Hotel with my date, the kind of girl you wouldn't bring home to Mother. In those days, the lounge was a very romantic place—roaming violinists, flaming torches, the works. Frank Sinatra happened to be sitting at another table with Lena Horne and a bunch of other stars.

I was trying to be a big shot and get in good with my date, so I offered to introduce her to Frank.

"Do you really know Frank Sinatra?" she said.

"Are you kidding, sweetheart? He's a dear friend."

I get up and walk over to Frank's table. "Frank, I got a favor," I say. "Could you come over to my table in about five minutes so I can introduce you to my girlfriend? It would mean a lot to me."

He says, "You got it, Bullethead." He always called me Bullethead.

Five minutes goes by, and he gets up and walks over to us, and, with a huge smile, says, "Hey, Don, how are you?"

And with that, I jump up from my seat and shout, "Not now, Frank. Can't you see I'm with someone?!"

## The Day My Act Was Born

LISA LAMPANELLI IS A MAINSTAY OF *THE COMEDY CENTRAL ROASTS.*

"Bring back the fat chick!"

It was only five words, but they changed my life forever.

The place, in Meriden, Connecticut, was a mediocre

crab-and-burger joint that hosted a stand-up comedy show. The crowd was full of food, half full of liquor, and devoid of civility.

To be honest, my set wasn't my best—having just started in comedy—and I did about fifteen minutes of jokes about my weight, my Italian family, and my current relationship.

As I introduced the next comic, I breathed a sigh of relief. I had made it through the set. But while watching the comic struggle for laughs, I heard that fateful line: "Bring back the fat chick!"

I froze. Sure, the drunken creep who yelled it was implying I was funnier than comic number two. But he had called me fat, a word that every woman from Eve to Eva Braun to Eve Ensler has feared. I felt my face turn red as the audience shifted its gaze to where I stood. In that instant, I made a decision: I was gonna get them before they got me.

I may be the only comedian who has been heckled when she was offstage, but in that moment, Lisa Lampanelli—Insult Comic was born.

## On Cruise Control

TOM PAPA WAS THE HOST OF THE *MARRIAGE REF* ON NBC.
It was my first time on the *Late Show with David Letterman*, and I was doing my best to control my nerves. After all, the crowd would be excited. Tom Cruise was scheduled. The problem was, that night Tom Cruise was pumped. Really pumped! He was trading-jokes-with-Dave and running-through-the-crowd pumped. I was doing my best to stay cool before going on, when Cruise ran offstage and made a beeline for me. He was sweating and breathing heavily like he had just won a prizefight. He grabbed my hand, locked eyes with me, and shook all his adrenaline into me.

"Whoo!" he yelled.

"Whoo?" I tried to say. I looked down and saw a drop of Tom Cruise sweat on my new suit.

He gripped my hand harder and screamed, "Kill it out there!" Cruise slapped my shoulder and in two quick leaps was up the eight steps to his dressing room.

I was now about to perform in front of a crowd of people who apparently filled Tom Cruise with pure rocket fuel, and I was freaking out! Making matters worse, David Letterman—who I'd totally forgotten about—was getting ready to introduce me. Me. Covered in Tom Cruise sweat!

Despite my brain screaming otherwise, my body went out and did the set without me. I don't remember much of it. The good thing about being a comedian is you don't really have to be there as long as the jokes show up, which, luckily, happened that night.

> "I was now about to perform in front of a crowd of people who apparently filled Tom Cruise with pure rocket fuel, and I was freaking out!"

## Soap Opera

JOY BEHAR STARS IN *THE VIEW* ON ABC.

Early in my career, I wanted to get into commercials, so I met with an agent. He took one look at me, and he said, "You're a good type for Ragù and Driver's Training Institute, but you can't do Procter and Gamble."

Then he reconsidered: "Well, you can do Procter and Gamble, but the blonde has to have the clean floor, and you have to have the dirty floor," which is ironic because you can eat off my mother's floor. We often did, since she could never decide on a dining room set.

## The Wrong Club

HEATHER MCDONALD IS A REGULAR ON THE E! NETWORK'S *CHELSEA LATELY.*

I was new in the business when a guy offered me a gig at his club in Santa Monica, California. When I got to the address and spotted the illuminated silhouettes of women flashing on the roof, I was energized. *This place really supports female comics*, I told myself. I walked to the door and announced to the bouncer that I was there to perform.

"Are you here for amateur night?" he asked.

Though I'd been doing stand-up for a year, I tried not to appear offended. He motioned to a waitress, who led me into the green room, where I met the other comedians. My first thought: *They're all so attractive. I wonder if they'll be telling jokes about being single and dating like me.* My second thought: *Why are they wearing only their bras and underwear?*

Suddenly, the feeling came over me that I had had once before when I was applying lip liner in a poorly lit bathroom at a T.G.I. Friday's and a man emerged from the stall—I'm in the wrong place!

They all think I'm a stripper!

Of course, I was flattered. Who wouldn't be? And when I found out the prize was $100, I considered entering. But then I remembered the high-waisted panties I was wearing and decided to stick with comedy.

## On the Cusp of Stardom

BRIAN KILEY HAS BEEN NOMINATED FOR TWELVE EMMY AWARDS AS A WRITER FOR *LATE NIGHT WITH CONAN O'BRIEN.*

Years ago, I got the opportunity to open for Jerry Seinfeld in Worcester, Massachusetts. There were four thousand people per show, and they were great. The next day, my wife and I came home to New York. Waiting for us was a message on our answering machine: "Brian, this is ABC TV calling . . ."

I began to shake. This was my big break.

"Your DVD player is ready."

Then we remembered: ABC TV was the name of the place where we had taken our DVD player to be fixed.

## The Day I Let It All Hang Out

CORY JARVIS IS A NEW YORK–BASED COMIC.

Before I was a stand-up, I taught English in Japan. A girl I dated suggested we go to a hot-springs resort. I said yes without knowing one crucial fact: I would have to be naked.

Walking outside the locker room, I realized something: No one but me was embarrassed. The Japanese are far more comfortable with nudity than the family I was raised in. When I was a kid, I walked in on my grandpa in just his underwear, and he still won't look me in the eye.

Sensing my trepidation, people began to make idle chatter with me, trying to put me at ease. I got so comfortable, I chatted back. I even got a couple of laughs.

Later, when I began doing stand-up, I realized that the hot-springs trip had prepared me for the pressures of being a comic. What else would help you get used to feeling like you're naked in front of a bunch of strangers who can't understand your jokes besides being naked in front of a bunch of strangers who can't understand your jokes?

## Best Heckle

TOM DREESEN IS A FREQUENT GUEST AND OCCASIONAL GUEST HOST OF THE *LATE SHOW WITH DAVID LETTERMAN*.

I was at a club trying out new material. Every time I got a laugh, some guy in the back would say something for a bigger laugh. I'd reply and get a laugh, then he would top me. After ten minutes of this, I finally trumped him.

"Just between you and me," I said, grinning, "I won that one."

He responded: "Just between you and me, you needed it."

## The Day I Won Them Over

JIM MENDRINOS WROTE *THE COMPLETE IDIOT'S GUIDE TO COMEDY WRITING.*

Right after 9/11, I performed for some relief workers. The audience was justifiably on edge, and I was just as nervous. What could I possibly say under the circumstances? How about the one thing that kept nagging at me?

I began by thanking them for working so hard. Then I said, "On that terrible day, New Yorkers asked two questions: 'Is everyone safe?' and 'I wonder if I'll have tomorrow off?'"

The relief workers laughed their butts off, and we had a great show.

## Learning to Be a Pro

ANDREA HENRY'S *THERE SHE IS . . .* WAS NAMED BEST COMEDY AT THE SENE FILM, MUSIC & ARTS FESTIVAL.

I was backstage at a talent-based reality TV show watching another comic being interviewed on camera. This, he said, was his last shot in the business. He had a wife, a baby, and one on the way, so he either wowed them tonight, or he was quitting the business forever and getting a real job. As he spoke, he choked up, and I saw a little tear well up in the corner of his eye. When he finished, the producer said, "Great! Now let's shoot it from a different angle."

After they readjusted the camera and lights, he did it pitch-perfect again, even the same little tear.

I Suck Up to Famous People

# The Funniest Person I Know: An Older Garry Shandling on a Younger Garry Shandling

**Putting together the *It's Garry Shandling's Show* for a DVD box set, I paid particular attention to the young star as he rambled on before the camera:**

"I go to couples therapy . . . alone. There are two therapists, and they argue about what's wrong with me." And, "I met a girl at a barbecue. Blonde, I think. I'm not sure, because her hair was on fire. And all she talked about was herself. Everything was, 'Help me. I'm on fire. Put me out.' I said, 'What about my needs?'" Because it was twenty-two years ago, and he doesn't look exactly like me, I had enough distance to think, *This guy's pretty funny*, forgetting that that *was* me.

Younger Garry was quick and upbeat. Older Garry tells dour jokes like, "I'm conservative on some things, liberal on others. I never burned a flag, but I never put one out."

Younger Garry also did a good job emceeing the *Emmys*, but the awards got in the way. Here's how Older Garry would improve those shows: Give everyone an award when they walk in, then take them away—one by one—during the night.

# Stop Clowning Around: Alan Alda Says the Joke's on You

**Here is Alan Alda's nightmare: He's at a party filled with fascinating, erudite people, men and women whose minds he would love to pick. But he can't.**

Why? Because some moron has him cornered, pelting him with joke after lousy joke—a ritual from which it's nearly impossible to escape.

Now, it's not that Alda doesn't like a good laugh. He loves a good laugh. And therein lies the problem. Whereas Alda likes his humor spontaneous and intimate, he finds jokes formulaic. And who are the main purveyors of this so-called art form? The same sex that "likes to take apart clocks" is attracted to "the mechanical formula of the joke." That's right, Alda's ratting out his own kind . . . men!

"You seldom have a woman walk up to you at a party and say, 'Stop me if you've heard this one,'" says the actor/ director (and author of *Things I Overheard While Talking to Myself*). That's because women tend to tell funny stories that let the other person in. "You won't believe the crazy thing that happened to me at the doctor's office today," they'll say. That kind of thing . . .

"It's actually more fun to tell a funny story than a joke," Alda insists. "Then it really becomes like cooking a meal for somebody and hoping they enjoy it with you. That's way different from the comic who's out there to kill."

Alda has a theory that men hammer away with the jokes because there's more simmering under the surface than simply trying to make the other guy laugh. "When I walk over to you and make you listen to me, and I deliver the punch line and you laugh, for just a second there's a power imbalance," he says. "It's like I've said I'm going to compete with you. And then you'll find it impossible not to come up with another joke. It's like two moose when they're young locking horns. A little bit of an invitation to joust and not just jest."

Here's another reason why guys tell jokes: Humor is a great aphrodisiac. Alda's alter ego, Hawkeye Pierce, was one of the great lady-killers of our time, which gives him an insight into why women dig funny guys. "There's the hope that if you have a sense of humor, you can be the butt of your own jokes. Or," he grins, "the butt of hers, which is higher up on the rings of paradise."

On the flip side, guys, the puppy dogs that we are, dote on gals who laugh at our antics. But what does that say about men seeking validation? "We need it a lot," Alda says, laughing. That's because there's a power imbalance here, too. Rumors to the contrary, women, he says, are the stronger sex. "Just think how strong you have to be to give birth." And men's claim to fame? A beer belly. Of course, "we can maintain that for more than nine months. In fact, for years. So maybe we are the stronger sex."

Well, then, what's a funny guy to do? Try being smart. "When you have a dozen people around a dinner table, it's not jokes that are prized," Alda says, "it's wit." And should that joke fail? Forget about it. "Oh, the deathly silence when the angel passes over. It's the angel of flop sweat. You really don't know what to talk about after a joke bombs."

Hearkening back to his nightmare, the actor, in his best borscht belt-ese, shouts, "Stop me if you've heard this!" And, cocking his arm back, he delivers a blow to the puss of his imaginary tormentor. "Pow!"

Now, *that's* funny.

# Oy, It's the Holidays!

Curmudgeon Fran Lebowitz explains
why she loves Christmas.

### The Holidays Growing Up

I loved Christmas. It was the only time of year that was
colorful, because the rest of life was a serious, black and
white world. And then there was Christmas, which, to me,
was dazzling—just the look of it. The town square was dec-
orated, and there was a Santa Claus house. I lived in a town
where there were relatively few Jews. And no one loves
Christmas more than a Jewish child in a Gentile town.

### My Tree-trimming Technique

I grew up with a girl who lived in this really big house with
a huge central hall and a tree that went up about, I don't
know, three stories. And my friend's mother and I had
wildly divergent tinsel-tossing habits. I thought you should
be meticulous about it, and she thought you should just
stand upstairs and drop it all.

### Why I Don't Shop Online

I don't shop online because I don't own a computer. My
belief is they haven't completed inventing them yet. Why?
Because they don't work. If they worked, not every business
in the world would have a department to fix them. They
don't have a department to fix pencils.

### The Worst Gift I Ever Got

My parents once gave me a carpet sweeper. And by the way,
I was in my thirties. And I didn't have any carpets.

# Mirth Mother: My Interview with Comedian Anita Renfroe

It began with some mother. The year was 2007. She was online watching a hysterical video of another mother breathlessly reciting a list of familiar momisms to the tune of the William Tell Overture.

"Are you hot? Are you cold? Are you wearing that? Where's your books and your lunch and your homework at?" She forwarded the video, "Mom-Sense," to a friend, who sent it to a friend, who . . . About fifteen million friends later, Anita Renfroe, the funny mother on that video, became a not-quite-overnight sensation.

"Getting the kids up and out the door, keeping them from bleeding or setting things on fire, and getting them into bed—condense that into two minutes and fifty-five seconds and it's a mom's day," says Renfroe, making sense of the video's popularity.

An easy laugher with three grown children, Renfroe, age fifty, lives outside Atlanta with her road manager and husband, John. Her new book is *Don't Say I Didn't Warn You: Kids, Carbs, and the Coming Hormonal Apocalypse*. We caught up with her to ask about her experiences in the 'hood, as in motherhood and womanhood.

**Andy Simmons:** Growing up, which TV mother did you want to be?

**Anita Renfroe:** Olivia Walton, because she was the one least like me. She was calm; she had lots and lots of kids, and being an only child, I thought that was kind of romantic. Until I had one myself, when I decided it was incredibly, incredibly painful. [Laughs.] To paraphrase Robin Williams, it was like getting a bowling ball out of an exhaust pipe.

**AS:** So which mother did you end up being?

**AR:** My children would tell you that my ability to win any argument would make me more like Clair Huxtable. But my disorganization and lack of housekeeping skills put me squarely in the Roseanne camp. So a hybrid—a verbal, undomesticated goddess.

**AS**: What pearls of wisdom did your mother pass down to you?

**AR:** Moisturize your neck.

**AS:** Excuse me?

**AR:** [Laughing.] Women always put moisturizer on their face, but they never get it down on their neck. And the skin on your neck is the same stuff as on your face, but it ages twice as fast because you don't ever put any cream on it.

**AS:** Makes sense. What else?

**AR:** When I was a self-conscious teen, she told me, "You think people are thinking about your zit or your large nose, but they're not. No one else is thinking of you as much as you think they are, because just think how much you're not thinking of other people." And she was trying to cheer me up!

**AS:** No doubt you imparted those bits of wisdom to your own children?

**AR:** Of course—on many occasions. There is something that comes with the mother mentality where you lose your mind and become like every other mother. I call it compulsive counsel disorder—the inability to not give advice all day long.

**AS:** The most famous mother in the world is Michelle Obama . . .

**AR:** . . . And with the best arms, oh my God.

**AS:** And she doesn't mind showing them off, does she?

**AR:** If my arms didn't wave back when I waved, I wouldn't mind showing them off, either.

**AS:** Have any advice for her?

**AR:** She's doing a great job without anyone's advice. I recall Michelle speaking to the press. One of her daughters interrupted. Michelle said, "Not right now, honey." But she smiled when she said it, and I don't think it was because there were a million cameras on her. I think that's her default face to her children. I love that. It seems that every time she speaks to them, it's with a smile on her face.

**AS:** What was your own child-rearing philosophy?

**AR:** I made it a point that laughter had to be a hallmark in our home. I wanted my kids to have a lot of funny stories to tell at my funeral. We didn't have loads of rules at the dinner table like many families, so there was a lot of singing, cross talking, maybe some chewing with your mouth open. But there was also lots of laughter.

**AS:** It sounds like mayhem.

**AR:** My son's friend once joined us for dinner, and he sat at our table horrified. Finally, he couldn't take it anymore, and he said, "Does it occur to anyone that no one is listening?" We laughed because we, of course, were talking and listening. We thought it was normal behavior.

**AS:** So you didn't keep too tight a leash on your kids. How about now that they're grown?

**AR:** Oh, no. See, I got the memo that says if you do your job right, they'll all leave. Woo-hoo! My hope was that my children would become independent, fully functional adults. But there is nothing more satisfying—or more heartbreaking—than to realize your child really doesn't need you anymore.

**AS:** You will say things most women won't. What are so many mothers afraid of?

**AR:** Mothers have been conditioned to believe that if we cop to a moment of weakness, it makes us less human or pleasant. It's the opposite. Talking about these things shows how much we have in common. And some of those things are annoying. [Laughs.] One woman e-mailed me, saying, "If you gave your child twenty-five positive affirmations for every negative . . ." And I'm laughing, like, *Who* *has time for twenty-five affirmations when we have four minutes to catch the school bus?*

**AS:** How do men react to your act?

**AR:** They ask, "What about the dads?" So I wrote a song for them called "Dad-Sense." It's just two lines: "Ask your mom, ask your mom." The guys don't laugh much, but the women love it.

**AS:** Your husband resigned from his post as minister of a church to become your road manager. Are you at each other's throats yet?

**AR:** John's a very tolerant, patient man, and I'm an excitable, spastic woman. Between us, a lot of stuff gets done. But on the road, we're together twenty-four hours a day, so on those days we're home, he'll go outside or to Home Depot to try to make me miss him.

**AS:** Your faith informs your humor. But do you think that when some people hear the term "Christian comic," they assume they'll be preached to?

**AR:** I'm sure some are wondering, *Are they going to take an offering?* But I can't imagine that going to my show would be a much different experience than going to a club, other than the fact that my humor is clean and comes from a place of hope and joy, not anger. When you come to one of my shows, you pretty much get the same thing as if you sat down at a Starbucks with me—except, at the coffee shop, you wouldn't get the big musical numbers.

# The Funniest Person I Know: *The Office* Writer and Actor B. J. Novak on Ricky Gervais, et al.

**So many people were the funniest person in the world to me at various points in my life.**

In college it was Mitch Hedberg, the late great comedian. I first saw him on *Letterman* with my girlfriend. He was rebellious and sweet. I remember one line: "An escalator can never break—it can only become stairs." Or, "I'm sick of following my dreams. I'm just going to ask where they're going and hook up with them later." I quoted him for weeks on end until my girlfriend broke up with me.

Peter, the caterer for *The Office,* is very funny. He believes that every item he has is there to increase your sexual prowess. He will create a narrative about who he thinks you're dating and how his vegetable soup will increase your stamina.

Ricky Gervais, the writer/actor who created the British *The Office,* is the most recent funniest person in the world to me. He gives me faith that you don't have to be crazy to be a genius. And he giggles—a laugh that I would be embarrassed to have. It's the most high-pitched squeal of delight. It's another no-vanity sign of his comedy because it's really an unpleasant sound.

Your sense of humor changes over time. I'm lucky that I keep meeting new people that seem funnier than the last to me.

# Acknowledgements

To begin with, I'd like to acknowledge the fact that my facility for concentration is nil. There I was, happily playing Minesweeper on my computer instead of working, when Neil Wertheimer, who was then a bigwig in the books department and is now an even bigger wig in our international department, asked if I wanted to put a collection of my stuff together. I was so excited I blew up.

I would also like to acknowledge what most people know about me: I'm lazy. But my editors, Courtenay Smith and Katherine Furman, are not. They kept at me to rework the material until it was as smooth as my bloated stomach after eating an entire lasagna. They badgered and needled, then needled and badgered, then badeedled and needadgered until the book was completed and I was left a desiccated pile of dust gathered up by the winds and left to tumble back to earth, where my wife collected me with a DustBuster, before adding a few drops of water, whereupon I was fully reconstituted, thus breaking the DustBuster because she'd forgotten to remove me first. And that's what I have to show for all my hard work on this book—a broken DustBuster. And I blame Courtenay and Katherine and their insufferable insistence on doing their job conscientiously and exceedingly well!

I would also like to acknowledge the obvious: My feet stink. Doesn't matter what I do. I could walk on a mattress-size Dr. Scholl's Odor Eaters pad and they would still reek. Nonetheless, a lot of talented RD editors have braved the stench long enough to foolishly encourage and edit me, before fleeing my little cubicle. This list includes our editor-in-chief Liz Vaccariello, Peggy Northrop, Tom Prince, Jackie Leo, Marcia Rockwell, Jody Rohlena, Lorraine Burton, Harold Clarke, and my cpoy etidor Ingrid Osthy. Thanks also to Bob Newman, George McKeon, and Jen Tokarski for making this book look so good, and all the others I've worked with at Reader's Digest. A sweller bunch there ain't!

Keep laughing all year long with . . .

# America's Favorite Magazine!

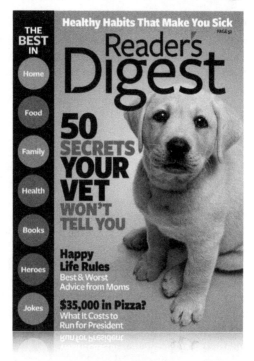

Now you can subscribe
every way you like to read!

# Get the BEST DEAL Now!
## RD.com/subscribe